A Region's Press:
Anatomy of Newspapers in the San Francisco Bay Area

INSTITUTE OF GOVERNMENTAL STUDIES
UNIVERSITY OF CALIFORNIA, BERKELEY

A Region's Press:
ANATOMY OF NEWSPAPERS IN THE SAN FRANCISCO BAY AREA

By

WILLIAM L. RIVERS

and

DAVID M. RUBIN

Department of Communication
Stanford University

1971

INTERNATIONAL STANDARD BOOK NUMBER (ISBN) 0-87772-072-X
LIBRARY OF CONGRESS CATALOG CARD NUMBER 71-631982
PRINTED IN THE UNITED STATES OF AMERICA
BY THE UNIVERSITY OF CALIFORNIA PRINTING DEPARTMENT

For Sarah and Tina

Foreword

More than two years ago the Institute conceived the idea of analyzing newspapers in the nine-county San Francisco Bay Area, with special reference to their treatment of public policies and community affairs. Perhaps more than in most metropolitan agglomerations, Bay Area residents have developed a substantial degree of community consciousness. Conversely, the region in which they live, with its broad Bay and numerous amenities, has acquired a high level of real and symbolic significance to its people. Treatment of the region's problems by the information media has been at least partially responsible for this image-building.

Consequently it seemed eminently desirable to examine the performance of the major medium through which public issues are discussed and opinions formulated: the region's newspapers. A research proposal was developed with the help of Harriet Nathan, and the regional newspaper study was added to the Franklin K. Lane series on Bay Area problems and issues.

William Rivers' unusual combination of training in political science and experience as a working journalist—plus his demonstrated analytic capabilities—gave him excellent credentials for his assignment. He has published numerous articles and several highly regarded books, including *The Opinionmakers* and *The Adversaries: Politics and the Press* (Beacon Press, 1965 and 1970, respectively). He is also an author, with Theodore Peterson and Jay Jensen, of *The Mass Media and Modern Society* (Holt, Rinehart & Winston, 1965); and, with Wilbur Schramm, of *Responsibility in Mass Communication* (Harper and Row, 1969).

Professor Rivers enlisted the aid of David M. Rubin, then a graduate student at Stanford University, and the work was begun. As the authors have indicated, the time periods selected for intensive reading and study of Bay Area newspapers were in late 1968 and early 1969. Like all human ventures, of course, journalism and the publishing business are subject to continual change. Much of this movement the authors have taken into account, on the basis of subsequent observation, interviews and correspondence. In any event, the "anatomy of Bay Area newspapers" prepared by Rivers and Rubin has far more than a temporary and local significance. The two authors have completed a very difficult assignment successfully and with distinction. In this they were aided by the generosity of readers, editors and working newsmen from throughout the area, who examined drafts of the manuscript carefully and made thoughtful and insightful comments on its treatment of the subject.

This remarkable response from concerned readers and newsmen who care about performance provided the authors with a wealth of information and viewpoints that were invaluable in the preparation of the book. It also indicated a deeply felt and widespread civic interest in how our newspapers do their jobs. Finally, the vigor of the response suggests that few things are closer to a region's conscience than its journalism, which thus may merit far more attention by scholars than it has yet received.

As far as we know, this is the first such study of a region's press. Perhaps it will help stimulate similar studies of other media, and of other regions.

STANLEY SCOTT
Editor

Contents

TABLES

APPENDICES

Introduction

Even in an era that is often called The Age of Television, newspapers continue to be the primary medium for transmitting substantial news and commentary on public events. We choose to analyze newspapers because it is doubtful whether anyone who cares about being informed can truly think of this as a television age. Granted that TV is the medium with the greatest impact, we are appalled by the brevity of television news reporting. How can two or three minutes of voice-over-pictures really tell us about Vietnam, or inflation, or the mayor's policies? Such reporting can, of course, give us the headline news, but not much more.

In addition, like too many of the headlines in your favorite paper, television often misleads. Indeed, we suspect that most television news—the illegitimate child of show business and journalism—not only fails to inform, but also actually distorts. No matter how dedicated to a truthful account of the day's events a television newsman may be, only through infrequent documentaries and special reports can he even try to inform us fully. He cannot transcend a news program system whose reporting is based on visual impact, a system dedicated to the proposition that a viewer's attention span is limited to one minute and 55 seconds.

The Bay Area has one program that attempts to offer more than the conventional television news fare: KQED's "Newsroom." It is valuable because it runs for an hour—a real hour, not the commercial television "hour" of only 48 minutes, with the rest of the time given over to selling soap. "Newsroom" is valuable, too, because it features reporters who know the news and can present it knowledgeably, without depending upon unseen scriptwriters. But "Newsroom" also points up some of the real limitations of television news. For example, viewers are forced to sit through all the reports that bore them, in order to see those they want to see. To a suburbanite who cares nothing about the activity in San Francisco City Hall, reports on city politics seem endless. More important, if one were to set into type all the words spoken during one whole "Newsroom" program, the resulting copy would cover less than two newspaper pages.

What the Authors Believe

So it was that we began our study of Bay Area newspapers with our primary conviction intact: *the newspaper is the basic news medium* for those who wish to be reasonably well-informed. We also undertook the study with other convictions, and with a full complement of biases.

1

Without attempting to distinguish the convictions from the biases, let us simply call them beliefs and sketch them here:

• We are political liberals. We hope that we are not doctrinaire, however, and that our opinions—on issues or newspapers—are not automatically predictable merely because we have liberal leanings.

• Whether it is called "backgrounding the news," "depth reporting," "interpretive reporting," or whatever, we consider it essential that today's newspapers go beyond the mere reporting of surface facts.

It should be said instantly that such reportage need not make a newspaper a grim instrument of determined education. We applaud the sentiments of the English publisher who said of American papers, "But they are conceived without sin, conceived without joy." We believe that a newspaper can be analytical and interpretive and still indulge itself in joy. We certainly rejoice in satire like that offered by Art Hoppe, Art Buchwald, and Russell Baker, in the humor of "Peanuts" and other comic strips, in many light stories fashioned by reporters and feature writers.

• We believe that the press must question and challenge government. As Abraham Lincoln said, "In this and like communities, public sentiment is everything." Without a challenging journalism, officials will too easily win public approval and influence sentiment. Moreover, at a time when most of the institutions of American society are involved with government, the press must question and probe into governmental relationships.

• We believe that the newspaper that attempts to report "society" news—i.e., the leisure activities of some local elite—wastes time, space and money, while injuring the community.

• Recognizing that few communities will support anything like the Los Angeles *Times,* we believe nonetheless that various kinds of newspapers must recognize their respective responsibilities to their communities. Some suggested responsibilities are outlined below.

RESPONSIBILITIES OF THE METROPOLITAN DAILY

The primary responsibility for a comprehensive report of international, national, state and major local news rests with the metropolitan daily.

The primary responsibility for interpreting (clarifying, explaining, analyzing) the news of the world, nation, state and central city must also rest with the metropolitan daily, which alone has the necessary resources.

If it carries out the above duties, the responsible paper will find it impossible to publish anything more than the most important news of the suburban cities. Moreover, the metropolitan daily that gives news space to minor meetings of clubs, civic groups, church groups and the like, however worthy the organizations or their purposes, cannot also fulfill its primary responsibilities.

RESPONSIBILITIES OF THE SUBURBAN DAILY

The suburban daily carries much the same responsibility as the metropolitan daily for providing its readers with world, national, state and city news—but its central focus and strongest emphasis should be on its locality.

RESPONSIBILITIES OF THE WEEKLY

The conventional weekly has reported the news of small towns and neighborhoods since colonial times. Such reporting is no less important today, because the metropolitan dailies and the suburban dailies, in the course of carrying out their primary responsibilities, must ignore the news of small communities and neighborhoods. The weekly remains the only medium for reporting the quality of everyday life.

The Hutchins Commission: Recommendations

Some of our own convictions grew from studying press criticisms, notably the 1947 Commission on Freedom of the Press, headed by Chancellor Robert M. Hutchins of the University of Chicago. Financed by publisher Henry R. Luce and the Encyclopaedia Britannica, the commission was composed primarily of academicians who had no journalistic experience. In its summary report, *A Free and Responsible Press,* the commission laid five demands on the press that still provide a useful starting point:

> A truthful, comprehensive, and intelligent account of the day's events in a context that gives them meaning.

> A forum for the exchange of comment and criticism.

> The projection of a representative picture of the constituent groups in the society.

> The presentation and clarification of the goals and values of the society.

> Full access to the day's intelligence.

Underlying the above demands is the assumption that an American citizen needs information—news of his local area, his state, his national government, the world—to be a responsible member of his community.

For those who have concluded their formal schooling, the newspaper (and interpersonal communication) used to be the primary sources of continuing education. Radio and television have in some ways usurped this traditional role of the press. The "Extra" is gone because speed is no longer a trait of the medium. At a minimum, radio and television are headline services and recent studies have shown that for increasing numbers of people this electronic headline service is quite enough. But most journalists, both working and teaching, agree that electronic news alone is inadequate and that the newspaper still has an important role to play.

Three Standards for Evaluating Press Quality

In translating the Hutchins principles into a workable method of press criticism, we have settled on three different standards for evaluating press quality. These are (1) objective reporting, (2) interpretive reporting; and (3) news judgment as reflected in the selection and emphasis of news stories in newspaper layout. Since we will be referring to these concepts frequently, we offer the following brief discussion of each.

OBJECTIVE REPORTING

Former *PM* staffer Kenneth Stewart, now Professor Emeritus at the Graduate School of Journalism, University of California, Berkeley, said of objectivity:

> If you mean by objectivity absence of convictions, willingness to let nature take its course, uncritical acceptance of things as they are (what Robert Frost calls the 'isness of is'), the hell with it. If you mean by objectivity a healthy respect for the ascertainable truth, a readiness to modify conclusions when new evidence comes in, a refusal to distort deliberately and be interpertive reporting, well and good. . . .

Philip M. Wagner, editor of the Baltimore *Sun,* contrasted objectivity with opinion, and stated that the distinction "is appealing in the abstract." He continued, "It also has certain practical virtues as a discipline to hotspur reporters, and in those cases where a publisher has the requisite qualities, it can yield brilliant results."

In brief, objectivity for reporter and copy editor is a state of mind, a point of view. It has many components: viewing a story in more than one framework, interviewing parties on all sides, considering and presenting all relevant background material, writing in an unambiguous and value-free manner, editing so as to include all important points of view and laying out the story so as not to embarrass any of the parties involved. No reporter or editor can be expected to do all this on every story, but the newsman should be aware of these strictures while reporting and editing.

We believe that a reporter's involvement in an important story does not make his writing objectively about it impossible or an unrealistic hope. Although journalism does not simply hold up a mirror to the world, the reporter can still be expected to write "impartially." As a guide, the standard of objectivity is useful. But it is not the sole determinant of newspaper quality.

INTERPRETIVE REPORTING

This is what the Hutchins report called "contextual" reporting, and it is frequently confused with opinion pieces on the news pages. Interpretive reporting—which aims to explain and clarify—is nothing more than a fact-gathering procedure intended to help the reader understand what he is reading. Former editor Carl E. Lindstrom stated:

> I do not know of an obscure or enigmatic or complicated situation in the news that cannot be explained by more facts. Facts—historical, circumstantial, geographical, statistical, reflective—can usually throw sufficient light on spontaneous news events to make them fairly intelligible. If this be interpretive reporting, well and good. . . .

Other newspapermen have stated that, considering the complexity of the world, the naked facts of a story are not sufficient to inform the reader. The facts must be buttressed with other facts from related stories: they require background. As long as the reporter's opinions are kept out of the backgrounding, the principle of interpretive reporting is acceptable to most editors.

NEWS JUDGMENT: SELECTION AND EMPHASIS

The third standard of quality lies in the choice of the news events to present from day to day, and the rather whimsical manner in which the stories are scattered about in the paper. Robert Fulford, book and art critic for the Toronto *Daily Star,* stated the problem this way: "In the papers, major stories are sometimes hinted at first, then blown up to flare headline size, then dropped to minor headline size, then eliminated entirely. The result is that readers can easily be left wondering whatever happened to the Suez Canal. . . ." Malcolm Bauer, associate editor of the Portland *Oregonian,* chastised reporters and editors for remaining "glued to the spot news break, the overnight sensation, the score of the game. They don't bother to look beyond the surface of an event—a surface that can be shown on television."

In amplifying Bauer's point, the Baltimore *Sun's* Philip Wagner was distressed that "no real distinction is made between hard news and the elaboration of meaningless and merely distracting detail. Worse, the real story can sometimes be missed even when it is there to be told, through this absorption in sensational diversions."

This type of reportage causes the reader, according to press critic Ben Bagdikian, to question the comprehensiveness and reliability of a newspaper. The reader should be able to feel after reading his paper that at least he has seen all the news developments on the major stories that day; that they have been properly tied to background material; and that, through the paper's layout, he has a feel for what are the most important stories. Too often a daily paper offers no sense of continuity or priority in the day's events.

The Bay Area Study

In reading and evaluating Bay Area newspapers, we gathered data in three different ways. First, we read as many editions of the papers under study as possible, plus as many of the weeklies and underground papers as we could track down. Naturally, we gave major emphasis to the metropolitan papers in San Francisco, Oakland and San Jose. Second, we interviewed executives and reporters of many papers, recognizing that the choice of interviewees greatly shaped our perception of the internal workings of each paper. Third, we used some quantitative measures such as column inches and story placement to give our admittedly subjective judgments a more solid foundation. (See App. IV for summaries of topics, newspapers and dates.)

We have presented our findings in a number of ways. We have drawn "personality sketches" of the 10 papers under study; we have made a special study of the Sunday papers; we have presented case studies illustrating press coverage of stories that posed great problems for journalists—student unrest and environmental deterioration; we have taken a close look at foreign news coverage and at the weekly and underground press; and we have commented on opinion columns. Our purpose has been to describe the accomplishments and deficiencies of the Bay Area press. We have focused on news coverage because that is the most critical operation for any paper, and we can justly be criticized for having given scant attention to special interests such as sports, business and society.

In addition to political biases and a predisposition toward the conclusions of the Hutchins Commission report, we have made many judgments along the way that we can only hope will become clear in the reading. It should be stated, however, that we have the greatest admiration for the working journalists in all parts of the United States. Confronted with explosive situations, and the target of criticism by successive national administrations, they are performing more capably than ever, under increasingly difficult circumstances. Our criticism is offered in friendship.

So many Bay Area journalists, former journalists, and academicians criticized all or parts of this manuscript as it went through various drafts that it is clearly impossible to name here all those who have helped us. It is possible, however, to thank two at Stanford who were helpful at several points: Diana Winter, who typed much of the manuscript, and Charlene Brown, who was a sharply perceptive critic, as always. We are also deeply grateful to Stanley Scott and Harriet Nathan, both of the Institute of Governmental Studies at the University of California, Berkeley, who encouraged us from the beginning, then proved to be excellent critics of the various drafts.

WILLIAM L. RIVERS
DAVID M. RUBIN

The Bay Area Press: An Overview

This book must begin with a brutal truth. As long as a publisher shows decent respect for a few laws, he may do what he likes with his newspaper. If he opposes the Democratic candidate for President—and he probably does—the candidate's name can be eliminated from the paper. If he hates golf, he can instruct his sports editor to forget that the game exists. If he visualizes thousands of little circles of family readers being offended by photos revealing the sex of naked animals, he can have his art department use an airbrush appropriately. The Democrats, the golfers and the artists on his staff may rebel, readers may protest, a rival paper may thrive as a result, but the publisher's power in such cases is unmistakable.

Freedom and the Publisher's Power

His freedom springs from the libertarian philosophy on which this country was founded: that every man should speak and write his own thoughts. The clash of conflicting ideas, the founding fathers believed, would produce something called the Truth. The concept remained popular during the period when any literate man could start his own newspaper with little more than a shirt-tail full of type. The concept lost persuasiveness as conventional production processes increased in cost and newspapering became big business. (Parenthetically, in an apparent return to the earlier pattern, low-cost photo-offset techniques have recently permitted a number of community and underground presses with limited capital to function as modern-day equivalents of the frontier publishers.) But even in the early days of the republic, the quality of information and amount of Truth available may not have produced an informed electorate. As we have since learned, men have ways of holding onto their attitudes and ignoring available knowledge. Thus, despite the hopes of the libertarian philosophers, it appears that our forebears were probably stunningly uninformed.[1] And now, in this

---

[1] We speak of a free press, but whatever its Constitution states, every society restricts free expression. These are the basic controls: a law designed to protect individuals or groups against defamation, a copyright law to protect authors and publishers, a statute to preserve the community standard of decency and morality, and a statute to protect the state against treasonable and seditious utterances. Although definitions of these offenses change, the U. S. Supreme Court has consistently upheld such laws. Two justices have nevertheless offered strong opposition to them. Holding that the First Amendment means literally what it says, Justice Hugo Black argued in *Ginsburg v. United States*: "I believe the Federal Government is without power whatever under the Constitution to put any type of burden on speech and expression of ideas of any

8

era of many single-newspaper towns, even the so-called free market-place of ideas is becoming but a dim memory, if, indeed, it ever existed.

As noted, individual publishers have great freedom to publish as they like. Fortunately, they do not take full advantage of their freedom. Whether this is because they fear the financial consequences of indulging their idiosyncrasies, because they want to avoid the professional condemnation of their peers and their employees, or because they feel a sense of social responsibility, most publishers give space to the Democrats and the golfers, and allow pictures of dogs and cows to run *au naturel*.

This does not mean that they are ultimately free and fair. In the beginning, publishing was controlled by the church, then by government, and now it is firmly embedded in the structure of business. Publishers maintain, usually correctly, that they are controlled neither by their business friends nor by their advertisers. They do not need to be. The businessman who runs a newspaper will nearly always understand the sanctity of the business ideology. His business is different from all the others—it is the only one specifically named in the Bill of Rights, and the color of the public interest is upon it. But even though his newspaper may question the morality of individuals—sometimes those in business, more often those in government—it is not likely to question the basic structure of either the capitalist system or the governmental status quo. Only fringe papers like the San Francisco *Bay Guardian* will probe into the distribution of money and power in society.

To ask any more of the conventional, commercial newspaper may be asking too much. When one considers the wide-ranging freedom the publisher has at his disposal, and the limited amount that he uses, it becomes clear that, according to his lights, he is socially responsible.

The Bay Area's Web of Papers

In overview, the nine-county Bay Area[2] seems to be awash in newspapers. It is served by 28 dailies (10 morning, 18 evening—a total daily circulation of over 1.6 million), plus 96 weeklies and over a dozen papers that are published monthly or two or three times a week, a few of them in exotic languages: Chinese, Portuguese, Spanish and Radical.

---

kind." Justice William Douglas has stated: "The First Amendment does not say that there is freedom of expression provided the talk is not 'dangerous.' It does not say that there is freedom of expression provided the utterance has no tendency to subvert. . . . All notions of regulation or restraint by government are absent from the First Amendment. For it says in words that are unambiguous, 'Congress shall make no law . . .'" (in *The Right of the People,* New York: Doubleday & Co., 1958; p. 21.)

[2] The counties: Alameda, Contra Costa, Marin, Napa, San Francisco, San Mateo, Santa Clara, Solano and Sonoma.

Since many of these papers appear fat (and profitable), one could easily assume that the nearly 5 million Bay Area residents are being informed up to their eyeballs.

But news coverage is not neatly geographic, with each paper covering its own ground. Nearly every newspaper pushes its circulation range as far as it considers financially feasible and then attempts to cover the news in the circulation area. In many cases, the result is thin coverage nearly everywhere. Not even the home city is reported thoroughly.

Holes in the Coverage

In one Bay Area community that seemed typical, less than 50 per cent of the public meetings of governmental bodies and civic organizations were attended by a reporter from the only daily in town. Some of the others were "covered" by making phone calls to officials and officers after the meetings, or by asking someone who planned to attend to call the paper if anything newsworthy occurred. What is more, the significant actions of many such meetings have apparently been obscured by seemingly endless wrangling, and a reporter's disposition might be improved by avoiding them entirely.

But this is a sure system for ignoring the threads that tie a community together. It is even worse. An official who is truly devoted to the public interest is frustrated in his best resolves by the absence of news coverage, while an official who is furthering his own interests likes nothing better than to pick up a telephone and act as his own reporter. One need not be a cynic to suspect that the absence of coverage promotes private interests. (A newspaper cannot leave it to radio and television to report such matters, and for the simplest of reasons: they do not.) The dilemma, of course, is that there are simply too many governing bodies and organizations, too many meetings.

It is futile to ask, of course, that the newspapers cover the Bay Area neatly in order to be thorough, one covering its own area intensely, another taking up where the first leaves off, and so on. This kind of orderliness is not even desirable. Not only do regional interests cross jurisdictional lines, but such a scheme would also force a reader to subscribe to all Bay Area papers to learn the news of the region. As it is, some of the most important regional stories are available in many local papers.

Diversity of Scope and Purpose

Duplication is far from complete, however, for another facet of the local newspaper complex is diversity of scope and purpose. Only five Bay Area publications—the San Francisco *Chronicle,* the San Francisco

Examiner, the Oakland *Tribune,* the San Jose *Mercury,* and the San Jose *News*—qualify as metropolitan newspapers. They are large in number of pages and circulation, seek to serve many readers in and out of the cities where they are published, and are designed to present at some length and in some depth not only local, regional and state news, but also news of the world. There is diversity within this group, with one paper playing up stories the others minimize or ignore. We will have much to say in later chapters about the distinctive personality of each of these papers.

The other 23 Bay Area dailies are published in smaller scope. Although they carry accounts of a few of the leading national and international events and supplement these with commentaries by syndicated columnists, their thrust is local. A few, like the Berkeley *Gazette,* pursue the minutiae of city life (Boy Scout meetings, PTA socials, descriptions of the season's tallest sunflower) with the avidity of a rural weekly. Most of the other dailies tend to leave such reportage to the weeklies and concentrate on reporting pivotal local institutions: city and county government, education, courts, businesses, churches, civic organizations and the like.

The more responsible editors of the surburban dailies are nagged by the fear that their readers can learn too little of the world from their pages. Elsewhere, such dailies feel that they can depend upon the metropolitan giants to tell area residents about national and international affairs, thus permitting the smaller papers to concentrate almost exclusively on local events. But many Bay Area residents subscribe to only one paper. Suburban editors believe that even the thousands who subscribe to a metropolitan daily and a local paper may not be adequately informed because Bay Area metropolitans provide such a slender diet of world news. In recent years, one result has been an increase in the world news offerings of small dailies, in some cases because the editors know that wire-service news is less expensive than hiring reporters to cover local news.

The Suburban Daily's Dependence on Wire Copy

It is worthwhile to sketch briefly how a fairly typical Bay Area suburban daily attempts to inform its readers. Virtually all of its state, national and international news is received from an Associated Press and two United Press International wires.

It is also worthwhile to consider how AP and UPI receive their news. Some of it is gathered by hundreds of wire-service staffers scattered among news capitals around the world. But as one Bay Area reporter pointed out:

The general circulation metropolitan newspaper is the chief news-gathering source for virtually all other news agencies. When I write a story ... a carbon copy is left on the AP spike. Another goes to UPI. At the two bureaus in the Fox Plaza, my story is perhaps given to a rewrite-man who may or may not check the facts further. The story then moves to the radio wire, the state wire, and, perhaps, the national wire.

That's how the Richmond *Independent* knows that a Richmond man has just been convicted in federal court. That's how a classical music station can report, in its five minutes of rip-and-read news every hour, that another conscientious objector has just gotten five years at Terminal Island. That's how the Berkeley *Tribe* discovers that the Establishment has struck again. That's how *Time* magazine learns that the son of a prominent New England minister has just been sentenced.

At the suburban daily, all the news is processed by a news editor and his two assistants. Besides making decisions on more than 100,000 words that come over these wires every day, these three men also edit and place all local news, which may run as high as 10,000 words a day, and select a dozen or so world news pictures from approximately 100 provided by a wirephoto machine every day. In this way, the three editors make up the general news columns.

The news editor does much of the work himself, discarding large quantities of wire copy and dividing the remaining stories among his assistants' desks and his own. Because all wire copy is received on punched tape (facilitating automated reproduction) as well as in type-script, editing consists largely of choosing between the AP and UPI versions of a story, checking for accuracy and typographical errors, and finding suitable points where stories can be cut. The punched tape can be set into type rapidly and inexpensively if few changes are made, and very rapidly and inexpensively if no changes are made. These are strong arguments against thoughtful editing.

Many a metropolitan news operation sneers at such standards. The great newspapers, and some of the merely good ones, combine the best elements of several wire service stories in preparing a single story. They set their rewritemen to work checking out wire service reports—calls to points across the U. S. and overseas are frequent, and travel by re-porters to the scene of breaking news is fairly common—and in general subject the reports of wire services and special news services to scrutiny and change. Instead of the two basic wire services that are common in small daily offices, a large metropolitan paper may have 15 or 20, in-cluding special services like those provided by the New York Times and the Los Angeles Times–Washington Post combine. Many of their re-ports go through a checking and rewriting process; nearly all are heavily edited.

At the offices of the typical suburban daily, however, there is little rewriting, and little time for it. Thus when the suburban news editor arrived at 6 a.m. on one of the mornings when his work was being observed, he found approximately 50,000 words of wire copy. (The wire service cycle for supplying news to afternoon papers begins shortly after midnight. Thus, most news editors who start work during the dawn hours find many stories waiting for them.) He swiftly discarded all but about 8,000 words. During the next seven hours, as the wires continued to spew stories, the news editor and his assistants used more than 20,000 words of wire copy of a total of about 110,000 available. Much of it was useless because AP and UPI reported many of the same events. They edited lightly, wrote headlines, placed stories on each page, and then sent the selected stories to the composing room to be put into type.

They also edited and placed about 6,000 words of local news, and selected and placed 16 pictures. During the last hour of their working day, they prepared some material for the next day's edition—just as, yesterday, they had devoted the final hour to preparations for today's paper. During a single working day, then, they edited the rough equivalent of a small book. To emphasize the large quantity of material that must be processed quickly by daily news editors, and the short time available for their work, one can contrast newspaper and book editing. Where books are concerned, even after the author's final manuscript is in hand, a publishing house customarily devotes at least six months, and often a year or more, to editing and producing the finished work.

The Suburban Editor and His Doubts

This thumbnail description ignores some of the underlying doubts that afflict the suburban editor. He knows that many of his readers will already have read elsewhere some of the stories he plays up, and that other readers will have been satisfied with the top-of-the-news sketches of the same stories heard on their radios or seen on television. But he is concerned to provide for those readers who want more than they are able to get elsewhere.

Other questions and doubts arise. How much serious news can his readers take? How many of them will read yet another report on Vietnam, another story on the indecisive Paris peace talks, and still another report on the interminable battle between the President and Congress? On the other hand, is the editor adequately serving those who follow such matters intently—they may be few but important people—if he publishes five-inch stories rather than 20-inch stories?

Is the editor furthering the causes of rioters if he emphasizes their actions? Can a community really be informed if an editor decides to play down all news of conflict? If he answers the clamors of local critics and tries to balance stories of conflict with stories of cooperation, how many subscribers will actually read all the reports on the good works? If he boldly headlines a story of conflict, his paper will be accused of sensationalism. Reports on the New Morality—especially those using the language that is its hallmark—will offend some older readers. Failing to give adequate attention to it will persuade many younger readers that they were right all along in thinking that the Establishment press was stodgy.

Such are the demands imposed by the effort to inform and entertain a heterogeneous audience.

Thanks to court decisions made years ago, the suburban dailies now receive the same basic wire services (AP and UPI) that are available to the metropolitan papers. But they cannot obtain all the special services (such as the New York Times News Service or the Chicago Daily News Foreign Service) that most metropolitans purchase. Some of the special news services and some of the syndicates that supply news and features have contracts or "understandings," with metropolitan papers that shut out the suburban papers. The metropolitans argue that their survival depends upon their ability to provide features that are unavailable to their competitors.

This explains, for example, the dreary comic strips that appear in some Bay Area suburban papers. They are not offered because the editors believe that many of their readers will be enthralled by "Priscilla's Pop" and the like, but because the San Francisco *Chronicle* publishes "Peanuts" and "Bobby Sox" and "Dennis the Menace." The *Chronicle* will not permit its strips to appear in the suburban papers.

All metropolitan editors treasure the attractive comic strips, and some who discovered quite late which ones are attractive have used cash to wrest "Peanuts" and "Dennis the Menace" from the smaller papers, which accurately forecast the popularity of the strips when they were first offered by the syndicates. Small-town papers may be able to assert territorial rights in some cases, but their contracts with syndicates have a way of running out, whereupon syndicate salesmen draw up more profitable contracts with metropolitan dailies.

There are other hazards in the jungle of comic strip syndication. The editor who tries to jettison "Orphan Annie" because he and his staff are sickened by it soon has 40 irate readers calling him regularly at three a.m. to protest. So he drops "Buzz Sawyer" instead, only to be reminded on the first day of the strip's deletion that the publisher is a Navy veteran who dotes on Sawyer. The *Chronicle* was recently pushed by public outcry into returning the offbeat satire of the "Odd Bodkins" strip to its comic page. Later, it was dropped again.

Such are the problems of publishing suburban and small-town dailies. Like the metropolitans, these papers serve such a variety of readers— the leading banker in town and the janitor who cleans the bank, the college professor and the high school drop-out—that this variety would seem to be problem enough. But the small daily editor must cope with the appeal of the metropolitan paper that looms next door, and with the local weekly that nibbles away in his own backyard.

The Non-Dailies

In contrast, the problems of the weekly are quite different. This is also true of the semi-weekly or monthly, regardless of whether it is the conventional kind that has provided the United States with its grass-roots journalism for two centuries, or the relatively new kind that challenges aspects of the established order. These publications—"non-dailies" seems to be the only term that will encompass all of them— have one stark advantage over the dailies: a sharp focus. The focus may be geographic, expressed in reporting the doings of a small neighborhood or suburb or town. The focus may be ethnic or racial, concentrating on Mexican-American or Negro life, or the Chinese community. In any case, the non-daily does not try to be all things to all men. Its scope and purpose are usually clear.

The Bay Area has numerous non-dailies of many kinds. Mort Levine publishes several of the grass-roots types in San Jose neighborhoods and in Milpitas. Others are the *Pacific Sun* of Marin County, the *Bay Guardian* of San Francisco, the *Freedom News* of Richmond. They are examples of the challenging papers that seek their readers across a wide geographic range in the Bay Area, but aim at creating a sense of community among those who are irritated by the blandness of the conventional daily, or who suspect that the promise of American life has not been kept. Talking to those who publish such papers makes it clear that there are compensations for producing this kind of journalism.

Money is rarely the chief compensation. For every non-daily that produces a significant return, five get by only because the owner and most of his family give nearly all their waking hours to publishing. But there is a sense of dedication and accomplishment among these publishers that is hard to find in the dailies.

There remains, of course, the underground newspaper, which may be best represented by the Berkeley *Barb* and *Tribe*. Such publications usually begin as challenges to the established order, with some valuable muckraking articles floating in a sea of nude pictures and four-letter words. Because few of those who work on these papers have any real interest in reporting, the muckraking becomes thin and usually comes to be based on rebellion more than on investigation. This eventually leaves little more than nudity and obscenity. There have been some startling successes in underground publishing, among them the *Barb*. The public wrangling between the staff and the owner—which resulted in the birth of the *Tribe*—during the summer of 1969 revealed just how lucrative such an operation can be. It also revealed that, like the capitalist men of the commercial press, some of those in the underground are also money-conscious.

Ray Mungo, one of the founders of the news service that provided material to underground papers for a short period (the Liberation News Service), has written of underground journalists:

> Lots of radicals will give you a very precise line about why their little newspaper or organization was formed and what needs it fulfills and most of that stuff is bullshit, you see—the point is they've got nothing to do, and the prospect of holding a straight job is so dreary that they join the "movement" and start hitting up people for money to live, on the premise that they're involved in critical social change blah blah blah. And it's really better that way, at least for some people, than finishing college and working at dumb jobs for constipated corporations; at least it's not always boring . . . that's why we decided to start a news service—not because the proliferating underground and radical college press really needed a central information-gathering agency staffed by people they could trust (that was our hype), but because we had nothing else to do. (*Famous Long Ago*, Boston: Beacon Press, 1970, p. 8)

In *The Underground Press in America* (Bloomington: Indiana University Press, 1970), Robert Glessing of Cañada College in Redwood City provided a useful definition of the underground papers: "created to reflect and shape the life style of hippies, dropouts, and all those alienated from the mainstream of American experience." (p. 3) In one sense it can be said that underground newspapers are written *by* the alienated *for* the alienated. The papers that fit under the broad canopy of Glessing's definition are wildly diverse, but he categorized them usefully under two headings that spring from their principal functions: radical political and radical cultural. The short essays Glessing received (and reprinted) after asking an editor of each kind of paper to assess the future of underground publishing, may indicate the degree of headway each category has made. Lincoln Bergman of the *Movement*, a political paper, wrote cautiously and conditionally:

> Money is needed to survive. Individuals get caught up into images of individual, not group success. The phone is tapped, agents infiltrate the group.

And so the only chance for survival is expansion. The need to speak to other people's needs. The attempt to reach and learn from the people on the bottom . . . who are the people who have the power to make the basic change. (*Underground Press*, p. 164)

Allan Katzman, editor of the radical cultural paper the *East Village Other*, is notably more confident that the underground can work basic changes:

In a very short time the underground press will erupt to the forefront of communications in this country. It will be brought there less by a radical commitment to some abstract principles than to a radical commitment to various and sundry experiences of living. It will have done the things necessary for change without, hopefully, blowing itself and others apart to do it. (*Underground Press*, p. 168)

Perhaps there are other radical political editors who are more confident of success than Bergman seems to be; and there may be radical cultural editors who are less expansive than Katzman about cultural changes that loom. It is nonetheless obvious that the undergrounders have worked more—or more obvious—changes in culture than they have in politics. Glessing is convinced that the underground is responsible for sweeping change, and he is willing to list cultural changes, such as those occurring in styles of hair, clothing, advertising, music, sex, sports and education. But observers who demand evidence that the young affect the lifestyles of others, while they are establishing their own, need do no more than ask a barber who caters to older men how his business is doing or ask a designer whether hippie styles have influenced the dress of the wealthy. Or simply look at a picture of the long locks curling over the back of the mod collar worn by former President Lyndon Johnson.

Glessing is also convinced that the underground is markedly influencing the mainstream of American journalism. He pointed to several evidences: the undergrounders cover stories that are later covered by the conventional media; many writers and editors work for underground and overground media simultaneously; and conventional media are used by the undergrounders to create and perpetuate myths.

Such influences are indisputable, but there is much more to say about the impact of the underground on the mass media. Glessing indirectly pointed up one important influence in criticizing the conventional (and devoutly conservative) Berkeley *Gazette* for shoddy reporting: "Perhaps that is why the daily *Gazette* circulation slipped from 15,502 to 14,299 from 1962 to 1968 while the underground weekly Berkeley *Barb* grew from 0 to 60,000 in the same period." (*Underground Press*, p. 145) Nothing is more impressive to the commercial press than the popularity of some underground papers. When the circulation of the Los Angeles *Free Press* approached 100,000, the editors of conventional dailies began to invite its editor, Art Kunkin, to their gatherings to explain his magic.

It is impossible to measure the extent to which daily editors have pirated or adapted the ideas and practices of the underground, but both piracy and adaptation are apparent. Some of them now print Dr. HIPpocrates, the unorthodox physician whose medical advice column started in the *Barb*, and some print the work of Nicholas von Hoffman, Washington *Post* columnist who did not get his start in the underground but whose irreverent columns would fit comfortably in the most radical sheet. The *Chronicle* prints both.

It is much too early to predict confidently that the underground press will, like the minority party, succumb because its strongest appeals are taken over and diluted to the point of mass palatability. But that may be happening. What is surely happening is that some of the strongest underground papers are achieving "conventional" success—or at least disproving the radical dictum that financial failure is the ultimate consequence of serving Truth.

Bay Area college papers may be better examples of purer, if partisan, motivation. Largely contemptuous of the values of the conventional, commercial press, and at least a bit suspicious of the values of some of the proprietors of underground papers, many college editors use their papers to promote the causes of youth. There is some excellent, dispassionate reporting in college dailies, and there are also some examples of reporting that the editors fondly suppose to be interpretive. Some Bay Area college papers deliver many of their news columns as well as their editorial columns over to frank advocacy. Reading their offerings reminded us of the era of personal journalism in the American press of 150 years ago. Ironically, this may be a wave of the future. Some of the younger journalists who work for conventional dailies applaud, because there is a growing belief that so-called "mirror to the world" journalism is dead.

The Bay Area has demonstrated that it will support most of the grass-roots weeklies and some of the papers designed for ethnic groups. Carlton Goodlett's *Sun-Reporter,* which is aimed at the Negro community, is strong locally and has developed something of a national reputation. Several Chicano papers are doing well.

The more stable of the underground newspapers make a lot of money, but it is almost as difficult to explain the precarious financial condition of the little journals of investigative reporting, challenge and protest as it is to explain why the serious approach of the old *Chronicle* and the Western Edition of the New York *Times* failed. We wonder why the San Francisco *Bay Guardian* has so much trouble reaching all the readers who would seem to welcome its excellent investigative style. Why did the *Plain Rapper*, a Resistance paper that seemed to speak directly to the concerns of the large radical community here, have to limp from one financial crisis to another? It finally died in late 1969. Why was the late *Peninsula Observer* unable to establish itself effectively with the dissident college and college-age readers who made up most of its audience?

The radical community is large enough to make such enterprises work, and if their journalistic standards are unconventional, most of their prospective readers couldn't care less. It is possible that distribution, which requires organizational ability of the sort the Establishment celebrates and practices so well, is faulty. That provides part of the answer, but not all of it. The hippie vendors who peddle the Berkeley *Barb* so successfully are evidence that the unconventional press can develop its own methods of distribution.

How Are Bay Area Papers Rated?

How do Bay Area dailies compare in American journalism? Judged in terms of prestige and prizes, not very high. When polls of editors, publishers, journalism professors and Washington correspondents are published, no Bay Area paper is ever found among the top 10. In fairness to the smaller local papers it should be noted that they have little chance of coming to the attention of many judges, and are not so much low-rated as overlooked. Small newspapers can, however, compete fairly equally with the giants for some of the Pulitzer Prizes and similar high marks of journalistic accomplishment that are geared to more inclusive nominations and wider consideration, but local papers, small and large, have had little success even in these contests. Finally, interviews with the newspapermen who have settled here indicate that they are lured more by the climate and by the Pacific than they are by the prospect of finding a great newspaper.

It was not always thus. Decades ago, San Francisco journalism was considered an important stop, or even a permanent home, for an ambitious newspaperman. The half-dozen San Francisco newspapers offered Bay Area residents across-the-board variety.

In contrast, Los Angeles was not much. Voting over 30 years ago in Leo Rosten's poll (prepared for his book *The Washington Correspondents,* New York: Harcourt Brace & Co., 1937), Washington reporters ranked the Los Angeles *Times* third among "least fair and reliable" American newspapers (just behind the Chicago *Tribune,* and two places behind all the Hearst newspapers, which together took first prize for unreliability). The *Times* was then as well known for intervening in politics as for covering it. When Rosten asked which newspapers the correspondents would most like to work for, the Los Angeles *Times* did not receive a single vote.

During this same period, Paul Smith was beginning a remarkable era in San Francisco journalism by trying to transform the *Chronicle* into a western cross between the New York *Times* and the New York *Herald-Tribune*. In one solid study, *Makers of Modern Journalism* (New York: Prentice-Hall, Inc., 1952, p. 401), Kenneth Stewart and John Tebbel called Smith's *Chronicle* "easily the worthiest major newspaper on the Pacific Coast."

By 1970, the situation had changed dramatically. A survey by *Seminar* magazine (a quarterly review for newspapermen, published by the Copley Newspapers), rated newspapers according to a scale based on positive and negative answers from 180 respondents who included members of the working press, educators, students, public relations and advertising men. The scoring system gave a plus one for each positive response and a minus one for each negative vote. Although the survey appeared to be impressionistic and made no attempt to achieve statistical significance, the results were interesting as a general indication of opinion.

The Los Angeles *Times* was rated very high, ranking fourth among all the American papers considered. It received a plus 20 rating for fairness. The *Chronicle*, on the other hand, was 21st in rank and got a minus 13 fairness rating. At the extremes, the *Christian Science Monitor* (which carried a report of the survey on page five of its August 28, 1970 issue) was top-rated with a plus 85, and the Chicago *Tribune* low-rated with a minus 52.

These bits of history point to a paradox. For today the *Times* of garish, metropolitan Los Angeles is further reputed to be the most improved newspaper in America, a worthy rival of the Washington *Post*, the *Wall Street Journal* and the St. Louis *Post-Dispatch*. It is now one of the most profitable papers in the world, publishing more news and more advertising than any other. The *Chronicle* of urbane, sophisticated San Francisco seems to be playing in a different league—one critic has suggested that it take on again the name that it had in 1865: the *Daily Dramatic Chronicle*. But in the years before its marriage of convenience with the San Francisco *Examiner*, the *Chronicle*'s circulation crept up as its quality declined.

This is all very mystifying. The Bay Area has one of the most intense concentrations of higher education facilities in the world. It is the center of a complex of industries that demand highly educated people.

San Francisco is proud of its style; some of its suburbs are no less proud of theirs. And yet the Bay Area did little to support Paul Smith's ambitious *Chronicle*. One editor who was lured here from the East years ago by Smith's promise of "a machine gun in every typewriter" now declares that Smith's vision was "all a lot of hogwash." Nor did the Bay Area wildly welcome the Western Edition of the New York *Times* when it came here nearly a decade ago. True, it was not a reasonably exact facsimile of the real New York *Times,* but support for it was even slimmer than the paper. Subscriptions were scattered, advertising was slender and the Western Edition died.

A sketchy review of the past 10 years gives us an outline of the kinds of journalism the Bay Area will support. In 1959, San Francisco was not just the home of the *Chronicle* and the *Examiner;* it boasted four major dailies, two of them circulating more than 100,000 copies each, two of them circulating more than 200,000.

Outside the City, publishing was fairly pale in 1959. Oakland was a large city, and the *Tribune* had 205,000 subscribers. But the limitations of the *Tribune*'s resources were suggested by Joseph Knowland's many titles: president, publisher, vice president, general manager and editor. The San Jose *Mercury* and the San Jose *News* were still in the hinterlands. The suburban and small-city papers were docile. The Palo Alto *Times* had a circulation of only 29,000. The San Rafael *Independent-Journal* had only 25,000 subscribers, and the Berkeley *Gazette* listed 15,025.

Now, however, of the San Francisco papers, only the *Chronicle* has a healthy circulation, 477,000. Both San Francisco papers, linked in a joint operating agreement that has them splitting profits, have a combined circulation of only 682,000. In contrast, the combined circulation of the four San Francisco papers was 724,000 ten years ago, when the Bay Area was much less heavily populated.

The circulation of the Oakland *Tribune* has risen very modestly from 205,000 to 209,000. The San Jose papers have gained readers: their combined circulation was only 116,000 in 1959; 10 years later it reached 204,000. They now rank among the top 10 newspapers in the United States in advertising linage, and the new home of the San Jose *Mercury* and *News* trumpets their wealth. Some newspapermen speak of it as "the Taj Mahal"; some of the interior appointments would do credit to a bordello.

Most of the suburban and small-city dailies are thriving. The Palo Alto *Times* and the San Rafael *Independent-Journal* will soon double their figures of 10 years ago. Nearly all of the other papers of similar size in the Bay Area have experienced increases of at least 50 percent.

Some of the success springs from stronger journalism; much of it is attributable to population growth and redistribution.

❖ ❖ ❖

We cannot provide final answers to several of the questions posed by this survey of Bay Area journalism, but the character of the Bay Area —and the kind of journalism it supports—is central to our investigation. If much of our attention is given to the established papers, and especially to the large dailies, it is because they seem to hold the key to the success of all the others. In addition, of course, they have the larger scope and the greater potential for affecting the lives of millions.

What can justifiably be asked of all these papers is that, within limits set by finances and other circumstances, they inform the community through news reports, analytical articles and opinion pieces. If they can also entertain their readers at the same time, so much the better.

Combinations and Ownership of Dailies

Appropriate fare for a weekly magazine may be positively scandalous in a weekly newspaper; and what might go unchallenged (and unnoticed) in a full-length book may cause a Senate investigation if broken in the daily newspaper. Norman Isaacs, a vice president and executive editor of the *Courier-Journal* and *Times,* monopoly newspapers in Louisville, and President of the American Society of Newspaper Editors, has put it this way: "The American citizen has different tolerances for different means of communication. He has the highest tolerance for cute books; and the next for specialized magazines. But he has the lowest tolerance of all for a paper in a monopoly situation."

If this is true, then boiling points of readers in much of the Bay Area should be as low as those of Louisville subscribers with respect to monopoly papers. The big five papers in the nine-county region have set the pattern for a combination that is proving popular for owners of newspapers at all circulation levels. The *Chronicle* and *Examiner* have carved up the San Francisco market with their joint operating agreement. It is known as the San Francisco Newspaper Printing Company, Inc., and controls, among other things, the circulation and advertising for the two papers. The San Jose *Mercury* and *News* are both owned by the Ridder family (and are therefore part of a communications empire stretching from St. Paul to Southern California). The *Tribune* is alone in Oakland and the dominant force in most of the East Bay.

In addition to these three fiefdoms, clusters of smaller papers under a single publisher can be found with ominous regularity. Peninsula Newspapers, Inc. (an employee-held operation) owns the Palo Alto *Times,* Redwood City *Tribune,* and twice-weekly Burlingame *Advance-Star.* The papers circulate in San Mateo and Santa Clara counties.

In Alameda County, Floyd L. Sparks and Abraham Kofman slug it out; Sparks runs the Hayward *Review,* Livermore *Herald and News,* and Fremont *Argus;* Kofman has the Fremont *News-Register,* San Leandro *Morning News,* and Alameda *Times-Star.* Dean S. Lesher is king in Contra Costa County with the *Times and Green Sheet* (in Walnut Creek), the Concord *Daily Transcript,* and the Antioch *Ledger.* Leo E. Owens is the owner of the Richmond *Independent* and Berkeley *Gazette,* and Warren Brown, Jr., the publisher.

This brief description of the daily power enclaves in the Bay Area is not intended as criticism per se. The authors have found both good and bad journalism in the above papers, as well as in such single properties as the San Mateo *Times* and Santa Rosa *Press-Democrat.* There is no simple rule about newspaper quality based on single versus multiple or monopoly ownership. Much of the testimony against the Newspaper Preservation Act (which has made legal a *Chronicle-Examiner* type arrangement) is equivocal on this point. It is difficult, for example, to determine the degree to which San Francisco journalism has been injured by the merger. It is much easier to document the financial consequences of such an arrangement than it is to point to a specific story and say, "This would have been covered more adequately if the city had two independent papers."

Along with monopoly and multiple ownership, however, is the offsetting fact that large numbers of daily newspapers exist in the nine-county area. The 28 separate dailies serving the Bay Area are one more than in the entire state of Kentucky; eight more than in either Oregon or Alabama; and roughly double the number in Nebraska. There are enough dailies on the Peninsula, for example, to permit a roving reader to start in San Jose and purchase a different paper every 10 miles or so. Although the papers have carved the Bay Area into spheres of influence as neatly as the world's powers have done for Europe and Asia, a determined newspaperphile can get at least three papers a day in his circulation area. (Appendix I lists the 28 dailies, their locations, circulation and chief officers.)

The American Newspaper Guild in the Bay Area

The American Newspaper Guild has a foothold in nine of the Bay Area papers, including the big five.[3] Top minimums paid to Bay Area reporters rank near the top on a national scale. Publishers have been particularly stingy, however, in offering money beyond the top minimums established by contract after five or six years of service. For this reason, while the Bay Area attracts good young talent, it is not always able to keep it. Many of the better journalists move on to higher paying jobs, leaving more youngsters with promise and those who never made it. Minimums are said to be higher for Bay Area suburban papers than for papers with similar circulations in other parts of the country, because regional collective bargaining was born in the Bay Area 20 years ago. Credit is given to strong guild leadership and philosophy for parity of pay rates in the suburbs.

With nine of the 28 papers at least partially organized, the guild in the Bay Area is well ahead of its national average. Nationally, the guild represents only about 10 percent of all U. S. dailies, including 81 of the 229 papers with circulations of 50,000 or more (including Canada). Fred D. Fletcher, Executive Secretary, San Francisco-Oakland Newspaper Guild, said that there is little progress in organizing new units locally, mainly because

> Guild organizing usually requires a combination of good in-plant leadership, good outside expertise and a need resulting from employer error or stinginess. That combination has been rare in the Bay Area largely because unorganized publishers have grown smart enough to maintain salaries and other benefits that appear, repeat appear, to match what the Guild gets in Bay Area bargaining.

Fletcher emphasized that it is usually through mistakes of the employer that the ball for organization gets rolling, and not much is rolling at present. (See Appendix II for a selected list of papers around the country, showing reporter and photographer top minimums in guild contracts as of August 1, 1970.)

What Paper Do You Read?

One of the most intriguing questions (and one most difficult to answer) about newspapers in any region is, "How much difference does

---

[3] Papers represented are the *Chronicle* and *Examiner* (editorial and white collar staffs); *Mercury* and *News* (editorial, white collar and janitorial staffs); Oakland *Tribune* (editorial staff only); Richmond *Independent* (editorial staff only); Vallejo *Times-Herald* (editorial and advertising staffs); Santa Rosa *Press-Democrat* (editorial staff only); and San Mateo *Times* (editorial not including photographers and white collar staffs).

my choice of newspaper make to my perception of the community and the world? Or, does it matter which paper I read?" Setting aside for the moment such basic information as the size of the news hole (i.e., actual inches available for news or other material after the advertising inches have been sold) and the number of subscriptions to wire services and syndicated features, two quite contradictory observations can be made of Bay Area dailies in this regard: (1) As expected, there is a definable Establishment viewpoint in all of the papers, with a relentless, numbing sameness to the tone of coverage afforded the non-Establishment, such as student demonstrators, feminists, Black militants and other stereotyped groups. (2) Nevertheless, there are evident variations in what each of the papers feels is important both on a given day and over a period of months.

Comparisons, first of the *Chronicle* and the *Mercury*, and next of the *Tribune* and the *Examiner,* indicated the differences in news judgment among the area's top four teams of news executives. All the front-page stories, with the exception of local news items (which were different in each community), are presented below for each paper in three competing issues selected at random. Dates for the *Mercury* and *Chronicle* comparisons are January 23, 28, and 29, 1969; for the *Tribune* and *Examiner* comparisons, January 16, 17, and 30, 1969. Equivalent editions of the papers were selected wherever possible. Stories that appeared on the front pages of both papers are listed first. The page numbers in parentheses indicate where the competing paper placed a story that was not on the other's front page.

TABLE 1

NEWS JUDGMENT: FRONT-PAGE STORIES

January 23, 1939	
Mercury	*Chronicle*
Pueblo inquiry	Same
Flood tragedy—five die	Same
U. S. poor crippled by hunger	Same
Feeble support for San Jose State College teachers' strike	Same
Vote on Hickel due (6)	Fire at Wheeler Hall (not in *Mercury*)
Trustees eye talks with SFS (San Francisco State College) students (15)	Senate bill to end draft (9)
	Quiet UC strike (18)
	Appointment of Pete Wilson to state Urban Affairs Commission (2)
	Old guard purged in state Senate (2)

January 28, 1969

Mercury	*Chronicle*
Nixon's first press conference	Same
Reaction to Disney's Mineral King Project	Same
Pueblo inquiry (9)	
Southern California flooding (3)	(Remainder of front-page stories local to San Francisco)
Iraqi hangings incense Israelis (9)	
Archer wins the Crosby golf tournament (sports)	

January 29, 1969

Mercury	*Chronicle*
New Iraqi spy trial	Same
Peru seizes International Petroleum Company	Same
Nixon on crime and need for judges (13)	UC student violence (10)
Skiers snowed-in (not in *Chronicle*)	Nixon's new dog (3)
Reagan on flood aid (2)	California unions' drive to cut health costs (not in *Mercury*)
Lightning strikes United plane (not in *Chronicle*)	

January 16, 1969

Tribune	*Examiner*
Paris peace talks	Same
LBJ on wage-price spiral	Same
Two Russians in spacewalk	Same
Cabinet report warns of post-war recession (4)	
Repairs on the "Enterprise" (8)	
LBJ on breaking Paris deadlock (Not in *Examiner*)	(Remainder of front-page stories local to San Francisco)
Making an enzyme in a test tube (not in *Examiner*)	
Bomb found at SFS (not in *Examiner*)	

January 17, 1969

Tribune	*Examiner*
Soviet spacemen land safely	Same
Lack of funds haunts HHH (not in *Examiner*)	Cease-fire talks in Saigon (not in *Tribune*)

GI pullout seen by Lodge
(not in *Examiner*)

LBJ says Russ plug space-gap
(not in *Tribune*)

Washington courts asks
Garrison for evidence (10)

Reagan-Hayakawa in agreement
(not in *Tribune*)

San Jose professors get letters (5)

Rumor resigns in Italy
(not in *Tribune*)

SFS meeting (not in *Examiner*)

Nixon statement on Vietnam
(not in *Tribune*)

Regents sift independent study
plan (not in *Examiner*)

Jewish juror a problem for Sirhan
(not in *Examiner*)

January 30, 1969

Tribune	*Examiner*
Trouble at SFS	Same
Reds resist pullout and DMZ talks	Same
Allen Dulles dies	Same
Trouble at UC (4)	Jet raid charged by Iraq (5)
Pentagon to probe "Pueblo" (not in *Examiner*)	Philippine earthquake (not in *Tribune*)

The tallies from the small sample shown in Table I strongly suggest that differences in topics covered can indeed influence the reader's page one view of the world. In general, the *Chronicle* tended to give front-page space to U.C. activities, violent or otherwise. The *Mercury* put U.C. news on inside pages. The *Chronicle* emphasized San Francisco-based stories, while the *Mercury* gave more attention to non-local (i.e., non-San Jose) and non-California stories. In short, the *Chronicle*'s page one leaned toward local news with a dash of student-based violence, and the *Mercury* offered its readers primarily national and international news.

The *Tribune* and *Examiner* contrast showed even less overlap in the choice of front-page stories. Like its sister the *Chronicle,* the *Examiner* presented much San Francisco-based material, while very little on the *Tribune*'s page one dealt exclusively with the East Bay. The following qualitative discussions of newspaper performance explore these clues and tendencies more fully and examine the ways in which varying news judgments in Bay Area papers affect the focus and content of information presented to the reader.

Qualitative Sketches of a Ten-Paper Sample: Goals and Performance

In addition to asking whether and in what ways Bay Area residents were better informed if they read one paper as opposed to another, we also considered how well they were being served by the morning and evening papers in their areas. Over a three-month period, December 23, 1968 to March 4, 1969, we reviewed the performances of 10 dailies ranging in size from the *Chronicle* to the Berkeley *Gazette*. The sample included family papers, chain papers and papers with semi-absentee owners. The four morning papers in the study, (*Chronicle, Mercury, Gazette,* and Vallejo *Times-Herald*) represented 93 percent of the morning circulation (based on circulation figures from the *Editor and Publisher International Yearbook 1969*); the six afternoon papers (*Examiner, Tribune,* San Jose *News,* San Mateo *Times,* Palo Alto *Times,* and Santa Rosa *Press-Democrat*) accounted for 71 percent of the afternoon circulation. The 10 had the largest circulation in their respective fields.

The Metro Daily Papers

The performance of the five metro papers, i.e., the *Chronicle,* the *Examiner,* the *Tribune,* the *Mercury* and the *News,* is most important to the Bay Area community. As Joseph E. Bodovitz, Executive Director of the San Francisco Bay Conservation and Development Commission, has said, "If these five papers are not doing the job, there is nothing that can compensate for their deficiencies." The following qualitative sketches attempt to outline the philosophy of each paper, and to show how it has met its own goals and those of the community. We have tried to keep in mind the cautionary statement of one of the Bay Area's most caustic press critics, Bruce Brugmann, publisher of the monthly San Francisco *Bay Guardian:* "I put out a half-assed paper. It's the toughest thing in the world to put out a good one."

SAN FRANCISCO CHRONICLE (477,009[1])

Leaving Bardelli's restaurant one weekday afternoon, *Chronicle* executive news editor Bill German was approached by one of the paper's elderly readers, a San Francisco resident of prominent social standing. *Chronicle* film critic John Wasserman was then in the midst of a series

---

[1] Total circulation in 1969.

on the City's North Beach-nudie film houses, the text of which was often quite graphic.

"What is the *Chronicle* up to now?" the reader asked with a mildly reproving tone. Without waiting for German to answer, he continued, "I mean, you're a family, morning newspaper."

"If something offends you," German countered in a pleasant, off-hand manner, "you don't have to read it."

"You're all we have," the old gentleman said. "We have to read you."

Although the *Chronicle* does not straddle the Northern California market the way the colossal Los Angeles *Times* dominates the South, nevertheless it is easily the most important newspaper in the Bay Area (although not the most profitable). Its circulation is more than double that of its closest competitor, the Oakland *Tribune*. The merger with the *Examiner* left the *Chronicle* alone in the prestigious morning field, with only the South Bay's San Jose *Mercury* as competition in parts of the Peninsula. In Herb Caen, the *Chronicle* has the single most powerful columnist in the Bay Area; it has locked up most of the choice syndicated material, and it often has first pick of local writing talent.

More sassy than fat, the *Chronicle* has been lighting fires under San Francisco since the early 1950's. Publisher Charles Thieriot, editor Scott Newhall, managing editor Gordon Pates, city editor Abe Mellinkoff, and German seem to delight in making the *Chronicle* different from other metro dailies. One *Chronicle* executive has called it "the only aboveground underground paper in the United States," and he may be right. It is unlikely that there is another group of newspaper executives anywhere in the country—with the possible exception of those running the New York *Times*—that is so conscious of its audience, and of the effect of its newspaper on that audience. "Already conditioned to expect the unexpected from the *Chronicle*," German has written in a widely circulated memo, "the readers seem not even to be aware that they are being weaned into becoming readers of a more mature and responsible organ of information and opinion." Readers of the *Chronicle* do get a unique brand of journalism from a unique newspaper. Its responsibility and maturity, however, can be questioned on many counts.

The Circulation War

The *Chronicle*'s personality was formed in the great circulation battle with the morning San Francisco *Examiner*, a battle that raged from the early 1950's until the merger in 1965. Although it may come as a shock to some of the *Chronicle*'s newer readers, Scott Newhall's predecessor, Paul Smith, tried to fashion a heavy, responsible paper. How

close Smith came is debatable. He had a reputation as an excellent re-
cruiter, but no one on the staff knew what he wanted and the paper
was drifting. Newhall believed the paper "gave indications of being
self-consciously self-important. . . . The *Chronicle* had less coverage than
it has now, and a sense of humor was somewhat lacking."

In Smith's last year (1952) the *Chronicle* was third in circulation
in San Francisco with 154,608, trailing the morning *Examiner* (225,060)
and the evening *Call-Bulletin* (160,271). The evening *News* was fourth
at 125,625. The *Chronicle* also trailed the evening Oakland *Tribune*,
which had a circulation of 191,597. That year Charles Thieriot ap-
pointed Newhall to the editor's chair; his instructions were to make
the paper a commercial success. German wrote of the strategy of the
circulation battle as follows:

> What strength there was in the old *Chronicle* had always been with the
> upper level of the population, the upper level economically and intellec-
> tually. Home-delivered circulation was proportionally high. Street sales
> were low. Strategy and tactics called for attracting many non-readers of
> our egg-headish newspaper into our tent, and, once there, keeping them
> from drifting out again. It was also essential that our core of serious readers
> not be so disaffected by the raucousness of our new spiel that they pack
> up and go elsewhere.

Despite the concern for serious readers, the paper plunged eagerly
after circulation. The street edition received a daily banner headline,
which was "no longer reserved for the most consequential news of the
day." German's memo went on, "The banner, under its new concept,
was to be a piece of promotional advertising for the sale of that day's
edition, much in the manner of a headline on the cover of a slick
magazine." Typography was also changed. Leads were set in larger
type and white space around heads and pictures was increased.

Reporters were encouraged to reflect in their stories their own reac-
tions to an event, producing something German has called the *Chronicle*
"cult of personality." Newhall recognized the value of controversial
and readable columnists for building circulation; thus Charles McCabe
started as the "fearless spectator" dealing originally with sports, Count
Marco with unorthodox women's advice, Art Hoppe with political
satire, Ralph Gleason with jazz and rock, Herb Caen with his own
special material, and a number of others.

The most successful circulation builders, however, were a series of
wild pseudo-stories that often ran for weeks, providing the sharpest
contrast to the straight journalism of other Bay Area dailies. Jonathan
Root waged a campaign against poor coffee in San Francisco restaurants
under such banners as "A Great City is Forced to Drink Swill." Re-

porter George Draper covered a campaign to clothe the naked animals of the City, which led to the founding of SINA chapters (Society for Indecency to Naked Animals). The effort received nationwide play when Draper attempted to start a chapter in the U. S. S. R.

The *Chronicle*'s attempt to out-Hearst Hearst led to one of the funniest and most celebrated incidents in San Francisco journalism—one that proved how keenly competitive newspapering can be. In 1960 the *Chronicle* sent its then outdoors editor Bud Boyd into the wilderness of the Trinity Alps as "The Last Man on Earth." Boyd, his wife and three children were to be the sole survivors of a mythical H-bomb attack, trying to test man's instincts for survival. As the *Chronicle* asked on its front page: "Could an average city dweller exist in the wilderness tomorrow with little more than his bare hands?"

Daily dispatches from Boyd appeared on the *Chronicle*'s front page, including the inevitable "night of terror" in which Boyd fought for "survival against cold and exhaustion." At the height of interest in the series, the *Examiner* sent to the mountains a reporter who learned from "unassailable sources" that the Boyds had left their camp. At the campsite the *Examiner* found (and documented with pictures) fresh eggs, empty spaghetti cans, chipped beef containers, kitchen matches, coke bottles, and enough toilet paper to start a fire.

Examiner and *Chronicle* executives waged an editorial battle over the series, with Boyd and Newhall appearing on the *Chronicle*'s television station, KRON-TV, to present a "report to the people" on the episode. A masterful, closing touch was supplied by *News-Call Bulletin* city editor Harry Press, who assigned one of his reporters to test survival in Golden Gate Park surrounded by beautiful dollies, champagne and caviar. It had the whole town laughing.

Those readers interested in serious news coverage, however, were not laughing. The "Last Man" series was receiving major headline play in the *Chronicle* at the time John F. Kennedy was battling for the Democratic presidential nomination in Los Angeles. The Kennedy story took a back seat to Boyd's escapades. Further, the Boyd series had been syndicated to many other papers around the country, and several, including the New York *Herald-Tribune* and the St. Louis *Post-Dispatch,* dropped the story midway. The *Post-Dispatch* went so far as to denounce the *Chronicle* editorially for its duplicity, a rare event in newspaper circles.

With each series the *Chronicle*'s circulation went up 15,000, and German claimed the paper held about 10,000 of these readers after a series ended. By 1958 *Chronicle* circulation had jumped to 225,409, far surpassing both the *Call-Bulletin* and the foundering *News*. The

Chronicle trailed the *Examiner* by only 32,000. During the Boyd series the *Chronicle* finally passed the *Examiner*.

In 1959 the pattern of merger began to take shape. In only six years this process was to reduce San Francisco from four independents to two. The afternoon Scripps-Howard *News* and Hearst *Call-Bulletin* combined on a 50-50 basis, Scripps-Howard maintaining editorial control and Hearst running the business, advertising, production and distribution. In 1962 Scripps-Howard pulled out of San Francisco, selling its 50 percent interest to Hearst ownership and giving San Francisco two Hearst papers.

For the next two years the Chronicle Publishing Company and Hearst media giants continued to battle for the morning field in San Francisco. In 1964 the *Chronicle* topped the *Examiner* in circulation, 351,489 to 301,356. Although the Chronicle Publishing Company was and is in excellent financial health because of profits from KRON-TV, the financial condition of the *Chronicle* has been confused by the conflicting testimony of publisher Charles Thieriot. In a July 1967 statement at the Senate Anti-Trust Subcommittee hearing on the Newspaper Preservation Act, Thieriot said that with the exception of 1956, the *Chronicle*'s losses were of "modest proportions," and that not until 1964 was the *Chronicle* "breaking even."

Thieriot claimed that monies for fighting the circulation war with the *Examiner* were coming from KRON-TV profits. In a letter to Michigan Senator Philip Hart on December 11, 1967, Thieriot reversed his position, recognizing that the use of television station profits to drive a competitive newspaper to the wall might be damaging at license renewal time (as indeed has proved to be the case). In any event, he revised his analysis of *Chronicle* profits. Wrote Thieriot,

> Before depreciation, newspaper operations showed a small and manageable loss in 1955, a profit in 1956, somewhat larger but manageable losses in 1957 and 1958 and, as indicated above, a profit for each year commencing with 1959 through September 1965, with the single exception of 1962.

Clearly Thieriot wanted to make it plausible that the Chronicle Publishing Company was able to finance the battle with the *Examiner* out of *Chronicle* newspaper profits. Since publishers have historically been unwilling to discuss finances, we can only assume from the letter to Senator Hart that the *Chronicle* was not a failing newspaper at the time of the merger.

Circulation of the *News Call-Bulletin,* however, was down to 183,176, a drain on Hearst resources. Of the three papers in San Francisco in 1964, it is safe to say only that the *News Call-Bulletin* was failing. Although the *Chronicle* had a decisive circulation lead (and since the newspaper business is one of increasing marginal return, this lead would snowball), the *Examiner* still held the lead in the profitable classified advertising department. But the Hearsts thought it more profitable in the long run to end the fight. They arranged a treaty that would kill the afternoon *News Call-Bulletin,* move the *Examiner* to the afternoon and ensure its profitability, and give the *Chronicle* undisputed control of the morning market. Since the Hearsts already owned the *Examiner* and the *News Call-Bulletin,* it is hard to understand why they did not make the move unilaterally, without involving the *Chronicle*. The only answer seems to be the profit motive, the urge to insure a guaranteed profit by uniting the City's only two remaining newspapers. The same motive held true for the *Chronicle*. As the *Guardian*'s Bruce Brugmann charged, the *Chronicle* was willing to give up its independence simply for the higher profits "promised by a joint operating agreement that would destroy the need for expensive competition."

The Merger and Its Consequences

On October 23, 1964, the two companies agreed to form the San Francisco Newspaper Printing Company, whose stock was to be owned equally by the Chronicle Publishing Company and Hearst. The new corporation would perform the mechanical, circulation, advertising, accounting, credit and collection functions for both papers. The *Examiner* was to become an afternoon paper, the *News Call-Bulletin* was killed, and the two Sunday papers were combined into the single Sunday *Examiner and Chronicle*. The agreement was submitted to the Justice Department on August 30, 1965, the attorney general replying that he did not for the present intend to institute anti-trust action. On September 1, 1965, incorporation papers were filed in Carson City, Nevada, without fanfare, and on September 12 the agreement went into effect.

The major complaint of competing publishers against such an arrangement was spelled out by J. Hart Clinton, publisher of the San Mateo *Times,* before a Senate Anti-Trust Subcommittee on July 28, 1967. The committee was considering the Failing Newspaper Act (now the Newspaper Preservation Act), intended to establish definitely the legality of such joint operating agreements between newspapers. Clinton said that after the merger in September, the basic "open" display advertising rate for space in the *Chronicle* was almost doubled, from $1.20 per line in January 1965, to $2.32 per line. The *Chronicle's* increase in circulation as a result of the merger was only 33 percent, hardly justifying such a rate increase. The *Examiner,* with lower circulation and faced with competition from other afternoon papers (although not within the City) increased its rate from $1.03 to $1.55 per line.

On the other hand, a combination rate for advertising in both papers was set at $2.58 per line, only $.26 above the rate for the *Chronicle* alone. No other afternoon paper was available at a price of $.26 per line. This naturally led businesses to advertise in both San Francisco papers, making it more difficult for other afternoon papers published in the Bay Area to compete with the *Examiner* for advertising dollars. This arrangement would also surely preclude the start of a third competitive daily newspaper in San Francisco.

Already the merger has helped kill the San Francisco *Argonaut*, a semi-weekly "shopper" with a circulation of 200,000. The *Argonaut* folded in March 1969. Its final editorial stated that "One of the main factors in the suspension was a lack of interest on the part of a substantial number of San Francisco's larger retailers in supporting a new newspaper voice." The "lack of interest" was in part attributable to the combined advertising rate. Weinstein's Department Stores, which folded in 1966, currently has a suit filed in Federal Court against the *Chronicle* and *Examiner* for triple damages, claiming that the high advertising rates of the merger forced the company out of business. The head of advertising for one large, prosperous Bay Area department store chain has said, "After the merger we no longer had any leverage. With our bargaining position removed, we no longer get the position in the paper we want. They don't care as much about us as before." Although it was difficult for large stores to pinpoint effects of the merger, this advertising director, with 15 years' experience in the Bay Area, believed that the smaller stores such as Weinstein's and Hale's (which also folded) were hurt severely:

> With even two independent papers the small stores could advertise heavily in one at half the price charged by the merged papers. Now we *have* to take space in both papers, even though there is so much circulation overlap. If we just had another daily or even two independent papers, we could concentrate on either the morning or afternoon market. With the merger, we can't.

Classified ads have brought home the effects of the merger most sharply to Bay Area residents. Although it is possible to purchase a classified ad in only the *Chronicle* or the *Examiner,* such an ad is placed at the very end of the section in a column by itself. The ad is displaced from all the usual classifications (which location is the reason most people take out a classified ad) and dumped at the back. Thus one has to advertise in both papers, when in theory an independent *Chronicle* ad might be adequate. Further, the *Chronicle-Examiner* rate of $2.19 per line is $.15 higher than that of the Los Angeles *Times*, a paper with nearly 300,000 more subscribers.

The merger has hurt news coverage, also. No longer concerned about competition, the *Chronicle* locks up its paper around five p.m., with the exception of a few later stories for which the editors were prepared. Bay Area readers receive a morning paper that is closer to an evening paper in the currency of its news. The lack of competition has also produced what one *Examiner* reporter calls "a kind of indolence in the newsroom." Many of the reporters turned to outside, freelance writing because they no longer felt a challenge in daily journalism. "On a competitive paper," an *Examiner* reporter wrote, "a reporter's lack of zeal is exposed as soon as he writes a story that suffers by comparison with the opposition. On a non-competitive paper, nobody ever knows."

It is unlikely that the merger meant much else to San Francisco readers, who seem inured to monopoly and combination, from the actions of other industries, as well as from the newspaper business.

If old claims that only one paper would have survived a prolonged circulation fight are to be believed, then San Francisco is better off with both the *Chronicle* and the *Examiner* than it would be with either alone. The authors believe that the more media outlets under separate editorial control that can exist in a city, the better. The experience of other metropolitan areas suggests, however, that San Francisco could support both a morning *Chronicle* and an afternoon *Examiner*, wholly independent of one another. The publishers prefer it the way it is now.

A New Philosophy

With the circulation battle won, and its position as the largest and most influential Bay Area daily secure, the *Chronicle* then refined and expanded its war strategy into a fullblown philosophy of newspapering. As befits this electronic age, *Chronicle* editors thought of the news product in much the same terms as they thought of television: it must both entertain and inform. "The formula at the *Chronicle* calls for a combination of fact, truth and fun," German wrote. "Each edition each day should approach the goal of informing and entertaining most of the people most of the time." Newhall likened a part of his paper to a circus barker in front of a tent, saying "Hurry, hurry, hurry, the girls are just about to take off their clothes." Once inside, readers would find a story about Vietnam, or so ran the theory.

We noted during the study period, December 23, 1968 to March 4, 1969 that the *Chronicle* was edited to be read quickly. Readers could whip through most stories in a minute or two; placing the continuation of front page stories on the back page has speeded up the process even more, and has proven to be an innovation very popular with readers. But rarely did the *Chronicle* force its readers to tax themselves. The paper's news ethic, as city editor Abe Mellinkoff saw it, was "Will someone read the story? If the story is not read, it's not news." German believed that a good test of a story's news value was the likelihood that people would talk about the subject.

> We decided not to be any more bluenosed than the society in which we lived. When a topless bathing suit was first designed and debated, we fitted out a model in the first such suit and published her picture in a prominent position in the paper. We did draw the line at any print that exposed the nipples, but that was six or seven years ago.

The emphasis on snappy, lively, readable copy with eye-grabbing pictures is antithetic to the notion of the long-running series. The *Chronicle* runs fewer series than the other four metro papers because, said Mellinkoff, "a paper should be complete in itself." One *Chronicle* reporter said that it was "unheard of" for a reporter to be relieved of his daily assignments for a long-term story. The Wasserman series on nudie movie houses, another on homosexuals, and a third on life with Jackie Kennedy Onassis did appear in the *Chronicle,* presumably because Mellinkoff thought they would be read. They probably were.

The influence of the Norman Mailer-John Hersey personal style of journalism is evident at the *Chronicle*. The rather young, liberal staff seems to be given more freedom to experiment in print, in line with Newhall's "cult of personality." The *Chronicle*'s May 1969 coverage of the People's Park trouble in Berkeley was significant for its reporter-involvement with both police and demonstrators. Some informative and readable stories resulted from the arrest and incarceration of one reporter at the Santa Rita Prison Farm, and the attendance of others at People's parties and meetings. One *Chronicle* editor felt that Mailer's approach to an event, such as the March on the Pentagon or the Democratic Convention in Chicago, resulted in more meaningful reporting than did traditional journalism. "We're feeling our way toward a new method of communication in print," he said, "without the stereotypes of what a paper is supposed to look like."

The style of city editor Mellinkoff also contributes to the freedom of *Chronicle* reporters. Unlike many city editors, including Gale Cook at the *Examiner,* Mellinkoff does not exert tight control in assigning stories to reporters. He encourages them to generate their own ideas. Editing is also very loose at the city desk. Said one young reporter, marveling, "I got some stories past the desk that I never expected would make it through."

However, in the summer of 1970, some of the younger *Chronicle* reporters complained to management that they were unhappy about the goals and purposes of the paper. Although the dissidents would disclose little about the complaints, one said that the dispute was over the desire of the younger men to "publish a real newspaper."

Despite the Republicanism of its editorial page, the *Chronicle* has been the most sympathetic among Bay papers in its handling of the contemporary cultural scene, including hippies, drugs, sexual permissiveness and student unrest. Bernard "Bud" Liebes, who has worked for both San Francisco papers said:

> The *Chronicle* appears more liberal, tolerant, and "with it" on such contemporary issues, no matter how fleeting or faddish, as pop art, op art, rock, folk music, wife swapping, and foibles of suburban America. On all these the *Examiner* has been uptight, straight.

The mood created by editor Scott Newhall makes it possible for the *Chronicle* staff to treat such subjects in a way that William Knowland's *Tribune* or Joseph Ridder's *Mercury* staffs could never attempt. In a revealing interview printed by the Berkeley *Barb* on March 7, 1969—which Newhall called an accurate statement of his position—he described the relationship of his paper to the Establishment: "We have to play it cooler than you underground papers. We have to keep the Establishment anesthetized so they don't feel the pain as we stick the needle into their archaic veins and give them a transfusion."

Some Shortcomings

The hip philosophy of the *Chronicle* is as offbeat for a serious metro as the *Chronicle*'s many sins. Despite the lengthy gestation period each night, the paper is often a horror typographically. At least one major article every morning is so garbled with slipped lines, reversals, dropped letters and the like as to be almost unreadable. The authors are still trying to decipher the words "warth to lit" from a recent issue. Usually an afternoon paper, under tighter deadlines, suffers in its makeup, but the *Examiner* is much cleaner than the *Chronicle*.

Given its list of wire services and syndicated materials, the *Chronicle* should provide excellent national and international news and opinion pieces. Newhall has contracted for the services of AP, UPI, The New York Times, The Los Angeles Times-Washington Post and others. Editors of competing Bay Area papers charged that the *Chronicle* has bought territorial rights to these services (where possible) so that other papers cannot carry them. Moreover, they contended that the *Chronicle* uses only a fraction of this material, and often not the best. Although German occasionally runs a James Reston or Tom Wicker opinion piece from the New York Times as a front-page story (a valuable and exciting idea), the bulk of the news copy comes from the AP, UPI, and Times-Post services.

The *Chronicle* puts heavy responsibility on the wire services for all non-local news; the paper has no Washington correspondent of its own, and no bureaus abroad. Considering all that is good in the *Chronicle* news philosophy, its conception of foreign coverage is hard to understand. "We have a general disinterest in detailed coverage of foreign politics and economics," an editor said. "We think our readers are more concerned with whether or not they use saran wrap in Kuala Lumpur than with New York *Times*-type foreign coverage." (See pp. 141–148 for fuller discussion of foreign news coverage.)

During the period included in this study, the *Chronicle* trailed the *Examiner, Tribune,* and *Mercury* in covering the major, continuing national and international stories. Appendix III shows the *Chronicle* in fourth position among Bay dailies on presidential news from Washington, and on Vietnam. It trailed the *Examiner* and *Tribune* on congressional news, and the *Tribune* on the Spring 1969 mid-east crisis. More important, the figures in column 3 of Appendix III show that the *Chronicle* was least likely among the metros to run such stories in the front of the newspaper. The *Chronicle* front page was heavily local and featurish. Serious legislative, non-dramatic stories (the type that make the *Tribune* "dull") were pushed to the rear. On the Presidio "mutiny" trial, however, the *Chronicle* performed best of all dailies surveyed, and was the only paper to run the story frequently on the front page. It was the *Chronicle*'s type of news.

Joseph Lyford and Spencer Klaw, of the Graduate School of Journalism, University of California at Berkeley, compared non-local news offerings in the New York *Times* and the *Chronicle* from December 12 to 19, 1968, and found some startling omissions by San Francisco's leader. On December 12 the *Chronicle* failed to carry a story from Ralph Nader about the dangers of driving a Volkswagen—there are probably as many of the German cars in the San Francisco area as anywhere else in the country—but the paper did find room for a puff story from Detroit about the Ford Maverick. The next day the *Chronicle* omitted a story on the union of Xerox and CORE to help passage of ghetto self-help bills.

On the same day, 16 publishers of newspapers with the same joint operating agreement as the *Chronicle-Examiner* asked for congressional approval of the arrangement. Lyford read about it in the Oakland *Tribune*, which has regularly outperformed the San Francisco dailies on this touchy subject. On December 19, urban expert Daniel Moynihan stated that the poverty program was a failure because it had emphasized community action over employment. Moynihan had studied the San Francisco experience, but the *Chronicle* had nothing on it. A final example (among scores of others) from December 18 typified the *Chronicle* attitude toward serious domestic and foreign news. The paper failed to mention the fact that for the first time in 40 years an opposition party had been organized in Portugal to push for election law reforms, press reforms and an end to detention laws. What the *Chronicle* did carry as foreign news was a story from Bologna that 19 men had been arrested for giving female hormones to cattle, leading the townspeople to think they would become sterile if they ate the meat.

Although the loss of the late editorial cartoonist Bob Bastian to KQED's "Newsroom" was sorely felt, according to one *Chronicle* editor, the editorial page and the stable of Newhall-nurtured columnists remains strong. The paper's talented group of reporters is led by science writer David Perlman, Keith Power, Michael Grieg, Dale Champion, Michael Harris, Carolyn Anspacher, Harold Gilliam, Scott Thurber, Bill Moore and others.

The *Chronicle*'s obvious strengths make its weaknesses even harder to take. The Saturday entertainment page with the lengthy "After Nightfall" column by ad man Hal Schaefer is sheer puffery. The amount of women's page space devoted to news of the debutante-cotillion set is far larger than that given by other Bay Area papers. One city-side staffer reported that many female society writers were "frankly upset" with the tone of the society pages. They have been pushing for more articles on Black women's organizations, and on the sexual and social problems of American women. Publisher Charles Thieriot is interested in preserving the "high society" look of the pages, so they are fighting a difficult battle.

Plugs for local, cooperating businesses are also a *Chronicle* staple. A year or so ago the paper ran a contest to choose the Sultan of Yanuca, with *Chronicle* columnists as judges. Reporter George Draper sent back a series of stories about the adventures of the new sultan, each story containing a mention that Draper and the sultan flew Canadian Pacific Air. Why? Public relations officials of Canadian Pacific Air had cooked up the whole scheme and were footing air fare expenses. These indiscretions, such major problems as the absence of Washington and Saigon bureaus, and the sad state of foreign news coverage, made the *Chronicle* disappointing.

The Chronicle's *Potential*

Jerrold Werthimer, long-time journalism professor at San Francisco State College, has praised editor Newhall for providing a spot in his paper for every special public. As a monopoly paper in a sophisticated city, however, the *Chronicle* should also consider educating and elevating its readers, rather than merely catering to them. Newhall has given signs that he would like to move the *Chronicle* in this direction, if time and energy permit. "We have to educate the American people —gently, with compassion—to the fact that they are not infallible," Newhall said in a recent interview with *San Francisco Magazine*. "There's going to be a lot of trouble in this country. We are on the brink of what may be complete disaster. . . . People are trying to make sense of a senseless world. . . ."

Newhall has established the *Chronicle* as a successful barker. The people are in the tent, and they've seen the girls take off their clothes. It's time for the second act.

San Francisco Examiner (204,749)

Critics of the financial arrangement that binds together the *Chronicle* and *Examiner,* and 21 other sets of papers around the country, have focused their displeasure on the combined advertising rate, the economic rewards given to a failing newspaper and the stifling of competition from other daily or weekly papers in the area. Another frequent criticism was that such an arrangement might lead to homogenization of both papers, causing them to become indistinguishable in format and viewpoint.

The Examiner's *Image*

This has not occurred in San Francisco. The character of the *Examiner,* "grey lady" of the afternoon and foil to the *Chronicle,* is evidence that some editorial separation can be maintained between merged newspapers. The *Examiner* long ago adopted a sober, conservative, often ponderous approach to newspapering. To those citizens who are confused or outraged by the *Chronicle's* antics, the *Examiner* looks more and more respectable. Purchased in 1880 by Senator George Hearst, who turned it over to son William Randolph in 1887, the *Examiner's* affiliation with the chain has only heightened its dour and prissy countenance.

Usually a paper with such matronly airs is able to view its competition from a position of strength—occasionally tolerant of the upstart's indiscretions, often grouchy and always domineering. The *Examiner,* however, is like an aged mother-in-law who has been clapped into a rest home by a son-in-law who then refuses to acknowledge her existence. The *Chronicle* calls the tune in San Francisco, and the *Examiner* may now be too old even to jump. One reason is the high average age of *Examiner* reporters (45), due to three mergers and guild seniority requirements for determining retention of staff. The mergers have also left the *Examiner* with overlapping layers of Scripps and Hearst authority, with no clear control other than at the top, where publisher Charles Gould represents the Hearst ownership. Among the committee of executives are editor Ed Dooley, executive editor Tom Eastham, associate editor Richard Pearce, managing editor Rene Casenave, associate managing editor Josh Eppinger, and assistant managing editor James McLean. All have decision-making authority.

The Shift to the Afternoon

If this imagery has been unnecessarily harsh, it is only to show that the merger placed the *Examiner* in an impossible competitive position for circulation, although its profitability was insured by the merger. Thrown kicking and screaming into the afternoon market, after generations of competition nose-to-nose with the *Chronicle,* the *Examiner* has yet to recover psychologically from the change. "The *Examiner* had a lot of esprit before the merger," said city editor Gale Cook. "It was not a happy thing. We preferred being a morning paper—it is much easier to put out."

Even a cursory study of metro papers in the United States today reveals that the morning market is the stronger, so the *Examiner's* banishment immediately put it on the defensive. The "let-them-try-to-read-it-in-another-paper" attitude has also hurt morale at both the *Examiner* and the *Chronicle,* particularly among reporters who were accustomed to working in a competitive situation. Said one *Chronicle* reporter, "The things that made for good newspapering before the merger in San Francisco are gone. The professional reporters would like to go back to the competitive situation."

The logistics of an afternoon paper give the staff less time to put it out, compel it to struggle for new leads to top the morning paper, require the sports staff to concentrate on feature writing, since game stories are all prepared by a morning staff, and force the city and news editors to be acutely aware of how far the morning paper has developed a story. If the *Chronicle's* entertainment writers did not so often decline to review operas, concerts, plays and club performances until two days afterward, the *Examiner* would be forced into second position in this respect as well. (The paper does have it a bit easier than its Eastern cousins because of the three-hour time difference, but the wire services tend to operate with only Eastern deadlines in mind, creating another problem at Western afternoon papers.) Control of the Sunday *Examiner-Chronicle* was one tidbit yielded to the Hearsts, although even here the *Chronicle* exacted its pound of flesh. The *Chronicle's* contribution, "Sunday Punch," is entirely free of ads, while the "Datebook" and *This World* magazine have a few ads scattered about. The *Examiner's* sections, on the other hand, are loaded with ads.

Not content with banishing its rival to afternoon "Siberia," the *Chronicle* made the move with a comparative circulation edge of better than a quarter of a million. From its final morning circulation of just over 300,000, the *Examiner* dropped to 220,000 in 1967, continuing the decline to 204,000 in 1969. The limitations of the afternoon market made it unlikely that Examiner circulation would rise above 250,000, about half the *Chronicle's* size. This ceiling affected staff morale. Further, as indicated earlier, the *Chronicle* has contracted for the most desirable of the syndicated services. The *Examiner* was left primarily with AP, UPI, Chicago Daily News, Hearst Headline Service, and the London Daily Express, plus a few others. Editor Ed Dooley said he has all the syndicated opinion material he can use, but that he would surely like the *Chronicle's* Times-Post service.

"We're Out to Top Them..."?

The merger was wholly a marriage of financial convenience. "Any time we can beat the *Chronicle* we do it with glee," Cook said.[2] "We're out to top them if we can. It's one of our few small pleasures left." There is said to be an unwritten rule that none of the *Examiner* editorial people can go over to the *Chronicle's* editorial room. If they must get together, there is a no-man's-land in the middle. (The papers operate out of two buildings at Fifth and Mission, connected through a common print shop. The *Examiner's* building is new. The *Chronicle* building has not been changed from the days of the *Daily Planet* in the old Superman comics.)

Although the bitterness between some *Examiner* and *Chronicle* employees is evident—Newhall seems unable to speak of the *Examiner* in a civil tone, and the worst insult city editor Mellinkoff could hurl at a reporter was to suggest that his copy read like the *Examiner*—the

---

[2] One of the ways Cook's men top the *Chronicle* is by covering the city—especially municipal politics and government—far better than the *Chronicle* has covered it in years.

authors are unimpressed with Cook's desire to scoop the *Chronicle*. In one of the juiciest incidents since the merger, the *Chronicle* was caught tailing former KRON-TV cameraman Al Kihn with private detectives in order to gather information of a compromising nature. Kihn had filed a complaint with the Federal Communications Commission detailing the manner in which the Chronicle Publishing Company, holder of the broadcast license, was said to be using the station to increase the company's profits. The *Examiner* failed to cover this incident, which Charles Thieriot later admitted did occur. The paper has also failed to cover the entire embarrassing and significant episode in which the FCC refused to renew KRON-TV's license without a public hearing. Not until the hearings began did the papers make amends. Surely if Cook were serious in his expressed desire to best the *Chronicle,* this story and others like it would have been on the front page of the *Examiner*.

In testimony before the Anti-Trust Subcommittee of the House Committee on the Judiciary, holding hearings on the Newspaper Preservation Act, Stephen R. Barnett, Acting Professor of Law at the University of California, Berkeley, indicted the *Examiner* in its handling of the *Chronicle*-KRON-TV story:

> In all the time since March (1969), when the FCC ordered the license-renewal hearing, the only story I have been able to find in the *Examiner* was the six-paragraph article . . . run on Saturday afternoon, March 22—two days late—reporting the FCC's action. The *Examiner* completely suppressed the story of the order issued by the FCC on June 5 adding to the hearing issues, at the *Chronicle*'s request, the question of the "quality" of KRON public-service programming (a question that many San Francisco citizens might want to testify about, if they were aware of the opportunity). It completely suppressed the nationally reported story of the Senate hearing on June 12, involving the private detective allegations and the alleged "blackmailing" of Mayor Alioto. And the *Examiner* has followed through by suppressing all the subsequent developments in the "private detective" story—including the *Chronicle*'s public admission that it hired the detectives, and its justification of its conduct, and including the FCC ruling adding the private-detective question to the issues to be explored at the hearing.
>
> Such is the "independent and competing" voice produced by the joint-operating agreement that this bill would foist permanently on the people of San Francisco. Such is the afternoon paper to which Thieriot referred when he told the Senate Subcommittee that "The reader has been well served under the agency arrangement in San Francisco, most particularly the afternoon reader." And such is the journalistic conduct that leads to the question: How many other stories have they suppressed that we *don't* know about?

Partially offsetting these sad findings are the *Examiner*'s opinion columns written by Dick Nolan and Guy Wright. They are valuable additions to San Francisco consciousness, far surpassing anything the *Chronicle* has to offer in the way of serious commentary on local politics. Ken Alexander is one of the better local editorial cartoonists, and the *Examiner's* "Cartooning the Week" on Saturday's editorial page, with six of the best cartoons from both the U.S. and abroad, is an excellent idea that might be adopted by other papers searching for a weekend editorial format. Some of the foreign cartoons provided the only hints to the Bay Area of the way journalists in other countries viewed the United States. These views are often sobering. Matching the tone of the unsigned editorials, the syndicated columnists are in sum, right of center and rather ancient. Liberals include Carl Rowan and Max Lerner, while Henry J. Taylor, William F. Buckley, John Chamberlain and Bob Considine all represent the conservative view.

The paper has been much slower to react to the anti-war and related political issues of the day than has the *Chronicle*. In the two-week period studied, the *Examiner's* coverage of the Presidio "mutiny" trial never made the first four pages (see App. III). Despite occasional good stories (see Regents' meeting at Berkeley, pp. 116–117), the *Examiner's* coverage suffered for two reasons. First, the *Examiner* tended to emphasize strongly the numbers aspect of the demonstrations: how many days of class were missed, how many cases of arson, how many arrested. (See pp. 120–121) This was done in a regular box slugged "Campus Scoreboard," which ran in a prominent place in the paper, and the leads of the daily stories were often pegged to such statistics. We might say that the *Examiner's* detailed attention to statistics became, after a while, like coverage of a cricket match. Second, the *Examiner* city desk was not as flexible as that of the *Chronicle* in allowing reporters to write stories out of the ordinary, to adapt to the situation.

Some Advertising Practices

Along with the *Chronicle*, the *Examiner* is guilty of running advertising puffery that passes for news. Gene DeForrest's "Around the Town" column on the Saturday entertainment page is, like Hal Schaefer's, an obvious "thank you" to regular advertisers. Editor Dooley laid responsibility for this column at the door of the San Francisco Newspaper Printing Company, agreeing that it was not "news," and he included his paper's Saturday church pages in the denunciation. The *Examiner* laid itself open for an embarrassing situation by running an ad for Brooktrails Redwood Park, a land investment company peddling recreational homesites. In the body of the ad was the picture of a Mr. Donald White, identified as a "Financial Newspaper Editor." White was at the time the *Examiner*'s financial editor, but his position with the newspaper was not mentioned in the ad, and his connection with Brooktrails (other than as an endorser) was not made clear.

Dooley confirmed a practice noted by editor Bruce Brugmann in his May 10, 1968 issue of the *Bay Guardian*. It concerned the printing of legal notices for the City of San Francisco. The city charter specified, in Section 13, that the notices be printed in a paper with a "bonafide daily circulation of at least 8,000 copies." For the past few years the *Examiner* and *Chronicle* have traded off a contract worth $135,000 a year, but the *Examiner* has had it the past couple of years.

According to the terms of the contract between the city and the newspaper, the paper of record must print the legal notices in an edition of at least 8,000 press run. Instead of running the daily column of legal notices in all editions, as most publishers appear to do, the *Examiner* only printed them in one street edition of 18,000 to 20,000 copies. Normally copies of street editions do not get into San Francisco homes unless residents purchase them from a newsstand or vendor. Thus, under this arrangement, presumably upwards of 200,000 readers of the *Examiner* never had a chance to see the legal notices.

Nothing prevents the *Examiner* from printing the notices in the home edition also, but the city does not require it. The city charter would have to be changed to require the paper of record to publish the notices in all editions, or at least in the home edition. Thus it appears that both the city charter and *Examiner* policy are responsible for this practice. Although the *Examiner* was living up to the terms of the contract, no other paper of record surveyed by the authors (including the Oakland *Tribune,* San Mateo *Times,* San Jose *Mercury* and Berkeley *Gazette*) failed to run the legal notices in all editions. Even so, the *Examiner* contended that it lost money on the city contract.

The State of the *Examiner*

Critical readers of the *Examiner* believe it lags behind its city in thinking; others see it as the only "responsible" voice in San Francisco. Given the current corporate arrangement, it is doubtful that the *Examiner* feels any pressure to change either its image or philosophy. This is unfortunate, because it seems to have good leadership in the news room and many excellent reporters, including Harry Johanesen (who recently won a McQuade Award of $500 for a 10-part series on the Negro in California); Jerry Belcher; Alan Cline; Gerald Adams, Mildred Hamilton, and especially political reporter Sydney Kossen. Lynn Ludlow, also an excellent reporter, supervises the best minority training program in the Bay Area. The *Examiner* has hired 16 interns for three-month periods, usually followed by a month on the reporting staff. In 1969 alumni of the program were working at the *Examiner, Chronicle, Mercury,* Sacramento *Bee,* Las Vegas *Review Journal,* Hartford *Times,* and the *Sun-Reporter.* While the Oakland *Tribune* has also made an effort to hire and train Black journalists, the *Chronicle* and *Mercury-News,* the two papers that can best afford it, have been most lax in this regard.

Forced to shift for itself, the *Examiner* would surely become a more interesting and exciting paper, and perhaps a more influential one in the process. As things stand, it appears that the *Examiner* could "scoop" the *Chronicle* every day for two weeks, and a great many San Franciscans would neither notice nor care. Certainly not the *Chron.*

OAKLAND TRIBUNE (209,120)

It may be significant that the manner of gaining entrance to the city room of the *Tribune* sets the tone for any analysis of the paper. A burly private guard mans a sign-in desk in the lobby of the building with the green-roofed towers in the center of William Knowland's Oakland. He first phones for permission and then directs the elect past a diversionary elevator to another tucked out of view. This elevator goes directly to the fourth-floor city room and executive offices. Visitors are requested to sign in and out. In its security system the *Tribune* runs a close second to the Detroit *News,* which has put iron bars over its windows. The wide-open policy at the new San Jose *Mercury* and *News* plant may as well be from another country.

Relations with the Black Community

It is not unfair to say that the *Tribune* is wary, if not downright fearful, of what its city is now and what it may become in the next few years. A number of reliable sources have speculated that Oakland may be as much as 80 percent Black within the next five to 10 years. Relations between the paper and the Black community are already strained. How the *Tribune* adapts itself to the changing urban environment in the near future makes it worth watching by the rest of the nation's metropolitan press. (The Detroit *News* has already opted to focus on the suburbs.)

A major reason for the distrust many Oakland Blacks feel for the *Tribune* was the paper's handling of a Black boycott of white merchants in the ghetto in 1968. Black citizens, disturbed at what they felt was police harassment of Black youth, complained at an open city council meeting, but did not receive what they considered a just hearing. The boycott was designed as an attempt to force the white merchants to pressure city hall over the police harassment issue. The *Tribune* responded to the boycott with a front-page editorial from the publisher, William F. Knowland, urging white Oakland residents and homeowners in surrounding areas to help break the boycott by shopping in the ghetto stores.

Although the *Tribune* had a journalistic right to take such a position, its news judgment was occasionally clouded by its editorial stance. On January 2, 1969, for example, the paper ran on its front page an AP story out of Washington, D.C. by Gaylord Shaw, headlined, "Students Get Pay as Dropouts." Shaw described deficiencies of the Neighborhood Youth Corps project in Detroit, based on data from the government's General Accounting Office. The article criticized the method of selecting trainees and implied a misuse of funds. Without making any effort to relate this story to the local Neighborhood Youth Corps project, the *Tribune* left its readers with the impression that the Detroit experience was typical. The editors ran it on page one. Among other Bay Area afternoon papers, the *Examiner,* the San Mateo *Times,* and the Santa Rosa *Press-Democrat* did not carry the story at all. The Palo Alto *Times* had a much-reduced version on page seven; and the San Jose *News* ran it on page 15.

Admitting that his paper has taken "a hard editorial position" on racial matters, city editor Roy Grimm stated,

> We try to give fair and full coverage of race problems in our community. We are criticized by some segments of the Black community as being racist, but we certainly make an effort not to be. If we ever have been racist in their eyes, it was certainly not intentional.

The conservative Republican philosophy of the Knowland family, which has run the *Tribune* since 1915, has had much to do with the paper's attitude toward Blacks. Joseph Knowland, father of the current publisher and a former congressman, purchased a one-half interest in the paper in 1915, and assumed full control in 1939 after a protracted court case. Sixty-one-year-old William Knowland, who had a lengthy career in the U. S. Senate, including service as majority leader in 1953–54 and minority leader in 1955–58, now exerts a major influence on the paper. Grimm offered this statement on the sensitive subject of writing to please a publisher:

> I like to think that we rarely knowingly slant the news. We don't have the problem of not covering a story because Mr. Knowland is against it, nor do we cover a story because he is in favor of it. But the emphasis we give a story is something else. When a piece can be handled a couple of different ways, the influence of the Publisher plays a part.

Grimm rightly claimed one of the best records of any paper in the West in the hiring of Blacks. In 1969 the *Tribune* had three Black reporters and a Black photographer, and it has given many other Black Bay Area journalists a start. Some of the *Tribune's* Black alumni have worked for the Washington *Post,* the N.B.C. bureau in Watts, the AP Sacramento Bureau, and KQED, the educational TV station. In addition, the *Tribune* did hire reporters of Oriental descent, but apparently did not use their special talents, such as the ability of some to speak Cantonese.

The paper has not had any particular difficulties in obtaining information from the Black community, but Grimm conceded that his staff may not be getting any "real information" at all. "We can't put out a paper just for the Black population of Oakland," Grimm said. "We're selling a lot of papers in other parts of the East Bay. We've tried to cover Black issues, and we've never injected the racial question into a story. But we give no race indication unless we think it is important to the story."

Political Coverage: The Cranston-Rafferty Race

In the political area, Knowland's influence was evident in the *Tribune's* 1968 coverage of the Cranston-Rafferty race for the U. S. Senate. The following figures (compiled by Patricia Kramer for the San Francisco *Bay Guardian*) deal with the column inches devoted to each candidate on the news pages of the *Tribune.* The figures speak for themselves:

TABLE 2
CRANSTON-RAFFERTY: COLUMN INCHES
IN THE OAKLAND TRIBUNE
October 1968

	Democratic Candidate Cranston	Republican Candidate Rafferty
October 1–4	15	54
October 6–7	0	75
October 10–16	14½	63
October 22, 24–25	22	56¼
October 28–31	17½	80½
TOTAL	69	328¾
AVERAGE PER DAY	3½	16½

The Tribune *and the Suburbs*

About three years ago the *Tribune* changed its policy of trying to "outlocal" the smaller dailies in its circulation area. Until that time there had been two separate editorial departments: a city staff and a state-suburban staff manned by bureau people. The bureau news was put on three or four pages that changed with each edition. Where a staff of 25 formerly covered the Concord, Hayward, Fremont, Martinez, Pittsburg, Richmond, Livermore, Alameda, San Leandro, El Cerrito and Walnut Creek areas, only nine now handle that job. Nevertheless, conversion to a central-city metropolitan newspaper was rejected, because 90 percent of the *Tribunes* were home delivered, many to suburban areas. The new goal was to provide the important governmental news and cover the biggest stories from the neighboring communities, and let the smaller dailies live by providing the more detailed local coverage. "We're no longer covering places like Hayward as we once did," admitted Grimm. "If I lived in Hayward, I would take both the *Tribune* and the *Review*." The paper does maintain a San Francisco bureau, not in order to sell papers in the City, but to show Oaklanders that they are not missing any San Francisco news by subscribing to the *Tribune*.

News Judgment and Page Design

Although the *Examiner* and the *Tribune* showed substantial contrast in their choice of specific front-page material, in their general news policies and treatment of certain major issues, the differences were small. During the study period of February 17 to March 4, 1969, the two papers ranked second and third behind the New York *Times* in column inches devoted to the Vietnam war, congressional news, and the President (see Appendix III); the *Tribune* did the most consistent job of the big four in its Middle East coverage. The paper performed poorly with the Presidio "mutiny" trial story, running few stories—none of them in prominent places in the paper—and prejudicing the reader against the defendants with its headlines. Headlines on *Tribune* stories concerning Vietnam and the cold war tended generally to be biased (against communists, dissenters, and the like), but on non-ideological issues the paper reacted to subjects much the same as the *Examiner* and San Jose *Mercury-News*.

The front page tended to be a bit more crowded than that of the other four major papers. The *Tribune* averaged slightly more than 11 stories per front page in the period studied, with an average story length of about 13 inches. The *Chronicle*, by comparison, averaged nine stories per front page, the *Mercury* slightly more, and the *Examiner* slightly fewer. Front page makeup was a bit on the dull side, often with a patchwork effect. *Tribune* makeup showed little imaginative use of white space or pictures, and few, if any, dramatic horizontals and diagonals (formed by headline position). Repetition of familiar layouts contributed to the unexciting appearance of the *Tribune*. The *Chronicle* and *Mercury* suffered from the same problems, and only occasionally did the *Examiner* stimulate the eye, although the latter underwent a face-lifting in the closing months of 1969.

On the editorial page, the unsigned editorials gave about equal emphasis to national and local issues; many were of the safe, "worthy of praise" variety. During the period studied, the *Tribune* congratulated S. I. Hayakawa, J. Edgar Hoover, the late State Senator George Miller Jr., David Packard and the communications industry as a whole. The opinion columns, syndicated material and feature page cried out for higher quality, more decisive writing. In a typical week's offering, syndicated columnists contributed 23 of 29 opinion pieces on national topics; five were locally written by Al Martinez on featurish subjects, and there was only one locally written item on a political topic. (Martinez has since lost his column and been put on general assignment reporting.)

The paper needs to develop its own writers who can comment intelligently on both local and national affairs, especially in view of the syndicated pundits on the "Focus" page: Hal Boyle, William S. White, Roscoe Drummond, and Dr. Max Rafferty, among others.

Finally, the editorial page devoted an average amount of space to readers' letters: 25 inches a day.

Since March 1969, the *Tribune* has converted its Saturday edition from an afternoon to a morning paper to capture more weekend advertising, the Saturday afternoon slot usually being a waste to advertisers anyway. The Saturday *Tribune* uses only UPI copy because the Associated Press would not allow the *Tribune* to use only the Saturday morning offering without paying for the rest of the week at a price that seemed prohibitive. Since the function of the Saturday morning edition is to advertise the weekend sales to shoppers, the loss of AP copy may be of minimal importance.

The *Tribune* is the only Bay Area paper to offer a weekly (Thursday) fashion section that is entirely staff written. It was begun in March 1963 by fashion editor Nora Hampton, who is presently assisted by Karen Emerson and Doris Hjorth.

The Tribune *Overall*

In sum, the *Tribune* is better than its reputation. The discussion on pages 131–132 makes it clear that the *Tribune* and reporter Fred Garretson (now spending a year at Harvard University on a Nieman Fellowship) lead the Bay Area in coverage of regional government and environmental issues. In Ed Salzman the paper is fortunate to have one of the best political reporters of the Sacramento scene. When confronted with dissident students, however, the *Tribune* bristled. Day-to-day, the paper resembles the *Examiner* in its handling of local, national and international news and its conservative approach. Considering their respective communities, the *Tribune* is certainly no further behind its readership than the *Examiner*.

The motto of the *Tribune* is "A Responsible Metropolitan Newspaper." The overriding question for the paper in the next decade is: to whom must it be responsible?

SAN JOSE MERCURY (126,171) AND NEWS (77,532)

The mere mention of the *Mercury* and *News* to other Bay Area publishers is enough to set dollar signs dancing. The morning *Mercury* and afternoon *News* (plus the combined Sunday *Mercury and News*) are the most profitable papers in the Bay Area, and among the biggest moneymakers in the country. Beneficiary of this bonanza is the Ridder family, which also controls the flow of printed news in St. Paul (headquarters for the Ridder chain), Duluth, Long Beach, Pasadena and a number of smaller cities across the nation. The *Mercury* and *News* are second in circulation to the St. Paul papers, but are the biggest moneymakers in the chain.

The *News* ranked second among all afternoon papers in the U. S. in ad linage in 1968, the *Mercury* fifth in the morning field. This was against such competition as the Los Angeles *Times,* the New York *Times,* Miami *Herald,* Chicago *Tribune* and others. The papers are fat—from 60 to 80 pages during the week and over 200 pages on Sunday.

Behind the Bonanza

There are two good reasons for the Ridders having developed a gold mine in San Jose. First, Santa Clara County and the South Bay region is the fastest-growing section of northern California. Shopping centers and tract housing are now as common as old corner drugstores. Inexplicably, the electronic media have not kept pace with the expanding market, and television has yet to make its presence felt in local advertising. The Ridder papers, which have championed the unbridled (and often unplanned) industrial expansion of San Jose, have vigorously filled the advertising gap. Thus they are, without question, the sole major advertising medium in the area.

Further, the Ridders have spared no expense in hiring topnotch advertising and promotion people to capitalize on the situation. Advertising director Louis Heindel, marketing department manager Gerold Zarwell, and public relations director Dan Stern are among the best in the business. With snappy color brochures they have demonstrated that the metropolitan San Jose market is 300,000 ahead of San Francisco County in population, $2,500 ahead in effective buying income per household, and $800 million ahead in total net effective buying income. The same comparisons have been made with Alameda County. According to Zarwell:

> There is no marketing and promotion operation in the Bay Area like the one at the *Mercury* and *News*. Only the operation at the Oakland *Tribune* comes close. The *Chronicle* has never done much along these lines, and since the demise of the Hearst ad service, the *Examiner* doesn't do much either. In the last ten years, only the Los Angeles *Times*, the Milwaukee *Journal*, and the Miami *Herald* have done the sort of thing the *Mercury* and *News* has done.

Zarwell attributed the high ad linage to the papers' concentrated coverage of the market. He said,

> We have the feeling there is no other market in the country where a paper can give such concentrated coverage of value to the retailer. We offer 80 percent coverage of the greater San Jose area, and 90 percent of our circulation is in Santa Clara County. We saturate this densely populated region, which is why we're able to draw from retailers what we draw.

He pointed to two carbon copy shopping centers, Valley Fair in San Jose and Bay Fair in the East Bay. "Valley Fair is doing very well with *Mercury* and *News* ads," Zarwell boasted, "but Bay Fair must deal with the Oakland *Tribune*, Hayward *Review*, San Leandro *Morning News*, plus direct mailing of advertising circulars to get its message across, and they are still not doing nearly as well as Valley Fair."

The new plant that opened in April 1967 symbolizes the papers' prosperity. Located on a 25-acre site near Route 101, it is the world's largest single-floor newspaper plant, and was voted one of the top 10 new industrial structures of 1968 by *Factory* magazine. Surrounded by a 136,000-gallon lagoon and hundreds of olive, sycamore and magnolia trees, the circular main entrance is unusual and inviting, the city room spacious and quiet. The facility far outclasses those of other Bay Area dailies.

The Editorial Side

There is, by the way, an editorial side to this commercial operation, and that is where the problems are found. Although there are managing editors, city editors, news editors, editorial writers and sports editors for the two papers, nearly all departments have been combined: education, society, arts, sports, travel, real estate and photo, among others. The overall operation is run by executive editor Kenneth Conn, who is responsible to publisher Joseph Ridder. Although the city desks are in a competition of sorts (Paul Conroy, managing editor of the *News,* says competition is encouraged "as long as it doesn't undermine or degrade the other paper"), such important local beats as city hall are staffed jointly by the papers. To a greater degree than in San Francisco, there is but one editorial voice in San Jose. In addition, the two have a single, forced advertising rate. It is not possible to advertise in only one of the papers.

Although the papers have been successful at knitting together a consumer market region known as San Jose, they have been much less so at creating ties with the citizenry and the community of San Jose. This is in part attributable to the papers' news philosophy. National and international news from the wires are heavily emphasized; local news, except for sports, receives short shrift.

The papers subscribe to AP, UPI, New York Times, Los Angeles Times-Washington Post, and the Copley News services. They were able to purchase the New York Times service, in competition with the *Chronicle,* only because they carried it before the abortive attempt at a West Coast edition of the *Times,* and the *Times* offered it back to them before selling it to the *Chronicle.* Because the many ads open up a large hole for news, the papers are able, both during the week and on Sunday, to run much wire material of a background and interpretive nature that never appears in the *Chronicle, Examiner* or *Tribune.* For those interested primarily in national and international news—as are many South Bay and Peninsula university people—the *Mercury* and *News* are the papers to read. (This leadership was not evident in the major, continuing stories, as the data in Appendix III make clear. Here the *Mercury* was only equal to or a bit below the other metros in total inches printed and prominence accorded in the paper. It was with stories of secondary and background importance that the San Jose papers were in front. Further, one knowledgeable observer of the San Jose scene noted that, although they were not given page one positions, *Mercury* stories on the Mexican-American community appeared frequently and were treated in depth.)

The *Mercury* publishes special sections for Monterey, Santa Cruz, and San Benito counties; southern Alameda County; the Peninsula, or "north county"; San Jose; and a street edition, which is primarily a remake of page one. Much of the coverage of outlying areas is better than local San Jose coverage. San Jose news is almost always relegated to the front page of an inside section, rarely appearing on the front page itself. In the December 23 *Mercury* the Julie Nixon–David Eisenhower wedding was front page with pictures, but no state or local item was to be found. On the 28th an Apollo shot received three stories plus pictures, but again nothing local was on the front page.

Superficial Coverage of Local Issues

When something of a local nature did appear on the front page, however, it tended to be the holdup of a grocery store or minor arson at a school. Violence at San Jose State College was also front-page material. But informative stories on industrial expansion, city government, the San Jose bus company, the waterworks, the garbage company or any other repository of local power were curiously absent. (The local television station KNTV carried more on these subjects than the *Mercury* and *News*.) There seem to be many sacred cows in San Jose, although executive editor Conn said that "there are no more policy stories [those stories specially treated or omitted through executive fiat] in our papers than in any others," a backhand admission that the papers did indeed recognize untouchables.

The refusal of the *Mercury-News* management to permit any real investigation into local business or politics is only one of the reasons for superficial local coverage. There is a standard policy among *Mercury-News* editors to trust wire service reports over the stories of staff members. One disgruntled young *Mercury* reporter stated that it was common for editors to ignore a story turned in by a staff member until it appeared on the wires. Then it was likely to be bannered.

As the largest metropolitan daily near Stanford University, the *Mercury-News* was in an excellent position to report the challenge to the university system, student unrest and related topics, the sort of thing the *Chronicle* attempted to do at San Francisco State on occasion. But the papers failed to run anything of an explanatory nature on the testimony of Stanford President Kenneth Pitzer before Senator McClellan's committee investigating student disorders: the papers carried only the bare verdict in the trial of protestors who stormed the Stanford Research Institute in May 1969, and blocked traffic on Page Mill Road; and the papers have repeatedly ignored such Black speakers in the area as Stanford Professor St. Clair Drake.

On the other hand, the editors have carried stories on the influx of radicals into businesses, on the belief of a local school official that students would turn to hard drugs if the supply of pot is cut off, and on the activities of Stanford radicals. In short, the papers have appeared to show a preference for stories depicting the less desirable aspects of young people's behavior.

Policies on the coverage of stories related to Blacks were highly conservative. One reporter stated that the office staff was aware that "it must not go too heavy on Black news at any one time." Because the *Mercury* and *News* emphasized crime stories in local news, this was the way most Blacks tended to be portrayed to the white community.

Similar policies affected the hiring of Blacks. To the surprise of many staff members, early in the summer of 1969, management rejected a proposal from the guild for the establishment of a minorities training and hiring program.

Aside from these evidences of prejudice, the more general philosophy of newspapering at the *Mercury-News* also helps explain the weak local coverage. Conn stated that three of every five readers are relative newcomers to the area, with little knowledge of or interest in local affairs. Thus it was international news and sports that held the readership together. The papers were willing to cater to these natural interests, rather than to work at creating a community spirit through increased local news coverage. Conn was aware that at some point the papers would have to tackle this task, but for now the *Mercury* and *News* are content with the second largest sports staff in the state (22 full-timers plus part-timers), which covers not only professional teams, but San Jose State, Stanford, 13 junior colleges, and over 100 high schools. (The Los Angeles *Times* boasts the largest staff—40.)

Civic Boosterism

Joseph Ridder and his papers are identified with the civic boosterism which has lured industry to the area. New businesses and job opportunities lead to more readers and advertising revenue. It is a good formula. But an electoral upset of June 1969, in which two of the three candidates backed by the Ridder papers were defeated, indicated to both Conroy and local weekly publisher Mort Levine that the homeowner was tired of continued expansion. "Citizens of San Jose are fed up with the 'growth for growth's sake' philosophy which the *Mercury* has been pushing," says Levine, publisher of the Milpitas *Post* and the San Jose *Sun* papers. "Frustrated, taxpaying homeowners are turning against the *Mercury* for its close Establishment ties." Conn agreed that the papers may be losing touch with the readers. "There is no question that we are much too close to the Establishment," he admitted. "You don't keep a man on the police beat too long because soon he will start thinking like the police." Conn added that many readers have complained that the papers did not write often enough about the planning aspects of growth.

Despite the civic boosterism, the *Mercury* does have one of the best full-time environmental writers in the state in Tom Harris. Along with the *Tribune*'s Fred Garretson, Harris has been active in forming an

Academy of California Environmental Writers. His editors give his stories more column inches and prominence than editors at either the *Chronicle* or the *Examiner* give to their environmental material. Harris has been particularly active in writing about problems of air pollution.

The local writers on the editorial and feature pages of the two papers reflect the Ridder unwillingness to confront civic problems head-on. The *Mercury's* Leigh Weimers and Frank Freeman both write lightweight, entertaining, feature-gossip columns, as does the *News's* Dick Barrett. Only the appearance of Harry Farrell, one of the best regional and Sacramento reporters in the state, and Lou Cannon, who wrote some good pieces on the BCDC (San Francisco Bay Conservation and Development Commission) and Leslie Salt Company, added bite to the local opinion writing.

Cannon, author of the celebrated book *Ronnie and Jesse* (N. Y.: Doubleday, 1969), is now in Washington, D.C., representing three west coast Ridder papers, including the *Mercury-News*. Incredibly, Cannon is the only local man from the Bay Area reporting from Washington. The *Chronicle* and *Tribune* rely wholly on wire services, while the *Examiner* has Hearst bureau men on call, a service better than having no one, but not to be compared with a staff employee.

The Future: A Chance for Excellence

There are predictions that San Jose may be the second largest city in the state within 10 or 15 years. With their presently secure financial base, the *Mercury* and *News* have the opportunity to become editorially excellent, as well as commercially successful. *Mercury* city editor Ben Hitt termed his paper's role in the community as "the only centralized voice in an uncentralized area." It is currently the voice for the retailers and the industrial establishment. But for the weak confederation of people, housing developments, shopping centers and highways known as greater San Jose, there is no voice now.

The Suburban Daily Papers

SAN MATEO TIMES (44,776)

Sitting in his San Francisco law office, the president, editor and publisher of the San Mateo *Times,* J. Hart Clinton, could represent the archetypical absentee owner. Each evening he receives a pouch of financial statements for the paper, including operating expenses, payroll and major purchases. He also checks over a packet of editorial material, including letters from readers, canned editorials from a special service and editorial cartoons. From this he makes up the editorial page.

Canned Editorials

Canned editorials are a bad sign—a very bad sign, indeed. The editorial and feature pages were natural places for us to begin examining the *Times*, because they demonstrated the paper's disinterest in its community. The *Times* editorial page is one of the few in the Bay Area that would be unidentifiable without its logo, or trademark. (The logotype is the newspaper's name printed from a single plate of type.) The signed and unsigned material could as easily have appeared in North Platte, Nebraska, as San Mateo, California.

Clinton apparently has not assigned very heavy editorial responsibilities to his general manager on the scene, Harold A. Schlotthauer, or to managing editor George Whitesell. Because of what Clinton called "a manpower shortage," the paper rarely editorializes on local subjects "unless they are very important." The publisher indicated that unless he wrote such pieces, they might not be properly written, and since he is an active lawyer, in addition to being a newspaper owner, he had little time to write editorials. Instead he subscribes to the Reed Editorial Service, which sends him batches of opinion pieces representing one interest group or another. The editorials from which Clinton must choose, statements that speak as the voice of the San Mateo *Times,* were ill-formed, poorly written and embarrassingly inept to anyone who is familiar with a quality editorial page. They were little better than the "odd-fact" fillers used to plug gaps on the news pages.

During the period surveyed, state and local subjects comprised just under 50 percent of the editorials in the Palo Alto *Times;* 60 percent in the Berkeley *Gazette;* 40 percent in the Vallejo morning *Times-Herald;* 50 percent in the San Jose *Mercury;* and 60 percent in the San Francisco *Chronicle.* Only 7 percent, or 1 in 15, appearing in the *Times* were on local or state subjects. What did appear? Here are two examples that lack both depth and specific relevance to the community. The first was one of two canned pieces appearing on January 2, 1969.

New National Gallery

Opening of the National Portrait Gallery in Washington came six years after approval by Congress—time enough, surely, to be sure it is a good museum, and that's what Dr. Charles Nagel, director, insists it is.

"This isn't an art museum," he says. "We are a history museum."

Right. But like other paintings portraits are of widely varying quality. As Dr. Nagel observes, "the important thing is the sitter; we want to get life portraits of each by as good an artist as we can discover."

In the "superb neo-classic" Old Patent Office Building, the collection is guaranteed worth going to see. From George Washington to John F. Kennedy, every president of the United States is represented.

Nagel likes Peter Hurd's portrait of Lyndon B. Johnson even if Mr.

Johnson called it "the ugliest thing I ever saw" and rejected it. The work is scheduled to be placed on view in the gallery after its subject is out of office.

Copying Britain's century-old tradition of the National Portrait Gallery of Art, in London, the scope of the new gallery is not limited to governmental personages.

The portraits now assembled there—most of them borrowed for the opening show—include 168 Americans "from Pocahontas and Aaron Burr to Will Rogers, Jefferson Davis and Albert Einstein."

This editorial appeared on January 18, 1969:

Money Costs More

Interest rates continue an inflationary spiral of their own, but the public doesn't seem to notice. The "prime" rate charged by most banks has changed nine times in the last two years—six times since April, 1968.

However, the problem of containing inflation remains unsolved. If the Federal Reserve banks continue to make funds available to commercial banks, although at a higher discount rate, and commercial banks continue making funds available to their customers, again at higher rates, inflation will continue to take its toll until American goods are almost completely priced out of foreign markets.

This year the U. S. trade balance could go into the red if inflation is not halted. It came perilously close last year.

It may not be popular with the outgoing administration to propose budget cuts which could ease inflationary pressures.

News Blackout on Bay Fill

Clinton's law firm represents West Bay Community Associates, a partnership comprising David Rockefeller and Associates, Lazard Frères and Company, Ideal Basic Industries (Ideal Cement) and Crocker Estate Company. They own 10,000 acres of San Francisco Bay lands between San Francisco International Airport and the Santa Clara County line, and they have designs on filling these acres for tract housing.

Many of the cities of San Mateo County are notorious for the amount of filling they have permitted in the Bay and marshlands. The question of "to fill or not to fill" is a live one in San Mateo County—or at least it could be if the newspaper were any sort of community voice. "My own convictions on Bay fill are not precisely those of my clients," Clinton said. "If I express my convictions in the paper, it might look like it was coming from my clients. So we have decided not to express any opinion on the Bay fill question on our editorial pages."

This blackout was extended to the activities of former State Senator Richard Dolwig of San Mateo. A frequent proponent of Bay fill, Dolwig was at the center of the political negotiations surrounding extension of the life of the San Francisco Bay Conservation and Development

Commission at the end of the 1969 legislative session. This action was seen by most conservationist groups as essential to the preservation of San Francisco Bay. Dolwig first introduced a bill that would have emasculated the commission; under great pressure from his constituency he then reversed his course, completely revised his bill, and made it the strongest of any considered by the Legislature. But, ironically, because of his past reputation, the conservationists distrusted it, and supported instead a somewhat weaker bill that was eventually passed. Clearly the subject of Bay fill and the activities of Senator Dolwig merited some sort of comment from the San Mateo *Times*, yet by his own admission, Clinton chose to remain silent. Why run a newspaper?

The paper has no local columnist, even of the gossip variety. "I used to have the managing editor write a local column," Clinton said, "but it turned out to be lightweight, on innocuous subjects, and it was taking up too much of his time, so I relieved him of it." Finding a replacement is not high on his list of priorities. Days go by without the appearance of any letters to the editor. In aggregate, the *Times* devoted the smallest amount of space to letters of any daily surveyed. But then the paper might not have received many letters, since it so rarely said anything controversial about San Mateo.

Syndicated columnists from Paul Harvey on the far right, to Roy Wilkins, a moderate Black, appeared frequently, along with more feature-filler material than in any other paper surveyed. The *Times* regularly carried on its editorial and feature pages Leonard Lyons, "Medical Memos" from H. S. Herschensohn, "Today's Almanac" from UPI, "Quirks in the News" also from UPI, "Junior Editors Quiz," "Sheinwold on Bridge," "Mr. Mum," "Let's Explore Your Mind," and others similarly innocuous.

The Metro Leap that Failed

Clinton has a much different goal for his paper than do the publishers of the Palo Alto *Times* or San Rafael *Independent-Journal*. When the San Francisco *News Call-Bulletin* folded, Clinton hoped to transform the San Mateo *Times* into a metropolitan paper to capture the old *Call* subscribers. He added more wire copy, and at a cost of $50,000 a year brought in the complete New York Stock Exchange closings. Thinner than the *Examiner* and generally printing only four or five pages of wire news, the *Times* was hardly in a position to compete as a metro. Yet the effort kept it from being a successful local paper. The most original idea in the *Times* (although it did not originate there), is a Peninsula news page billed as a "second front page," (not an adequate substitute for comprehensive local reporting). Said Clinton,

"We tried to persuade people that they were getting all the local news and all the wire news. Perhaps we went too far in the direction of a metro and don't emphasize local news enough."

Because of the many regional problems with which the San Mateo area is involved—including BART expansion to the airport, Bay fill, air and water pollution and highway construction—it is imperative that a strong newspaper speak for San Mateo County. (Some readers of the Redwood City *Tribune* stated that their paper does so, but that it is limited by the smallness of its circulation and newshole.)

There are so many hospitals, schools, police stations and city halls within the *Times*'s circulation orbit that its transformation into a comprehensive local paper would be a full-time job. This is perhaps the course Clinton should take. Presently the paper is floating, not really meeting the needs of any constituency.

An Uncommitted Property

An editorial change would require an investment of time and money. (Clinton does not himself own the paper, but runs the *Times* for his late wife's family who own 90 percent of the stock.) Recently funds have been spent on mechanizing the paper, to the detriment of editorial quality. The *Times* has two computers in operation, and type is set by computer-tape. "We don't want to spend our money this way," Clinton said. "We would rather put it into editorial improvement, but just to keep pace with other papers we have to spend it. Returning to the basic editorial foundation of newspapering is hard to do." Until Clinton recognizes that the *Times* is a lifeless, uncommitted property, he will never get back to the "foundations of newspapering." Meanwhile, urban and environmental problems proliferate in San Mateo County.

BERKELEY GAZETTE (14,219)

Most of the time the *Gazette* left little doubt as to its personality—a small, local-news oriented, militantly conservative fussbudget. But then the intense, young, frequently witty editor Mike Culbert would come up with an excellent series or layout and mar the image. On three issues, however, the *Gazette* was predictable: Communists (under every bed), student demonstrators and drugs.

The *Gazette* is closely tied both structurally and financially to the neighboring Richmond *Independent,* an afternoon paper of 36,000 circulation. Warren Brown, Jr. is publisher of both papers; Leo E. Owens is owner. Neither lives in Berkeley. Nor is the *Gazette* printed in Berkeley; all the shop work is done at the *Independent.* Since it was physically impossible to print two afternoon papers in the Richmond shop, the smaller *Gazette* was forced to switch to the morning field on October 3, 1966, a day Culbert said would "live in infamy." The *Gazette* must compete in the morning with the *Chronicle,* while its real news rival is the Oakland *Tribune.*

The shift to the morning, and a subsequent loss of 2,500 readers put the *Gazette* in the red, with the *Independent* covering its losses. Only in the fall of 1968 did the *Gazette* once again show a profit, but Culbert indicated he is still working on a shoestring.

As its puny 14,000 circulation in a city of 120,000 indicates, the *Gazette* is by Culbert's own admission, seriously "out of tune with the Berkeley environment." Culbert has found five distinct communities in his circulation area, only one of which is sympathetic to the *Gazette.* Three groups—the transient University student-faculty community, the more permanent faculty and staff residents, and a large, white, liberal-left group—are either simply not interested in the *Gazette* or at odds with its editorial philosophy. The same is true for the Negro community. The conservative, 1930's-type Berkeley holdovers are the paper's sole source of strength. The *Gazette* also circulates in the Albany, Kensington and El Cerrito areas, which creates a bit of a coverage problem for Culbert, who cannot afford to publish two editions.

When Owens took over the *Gazette* in 1966 from Berkeley resident George Dunscomb, the hope was to convert the paper into a metro-like, international newspaper. "I think the idea was absurd," said Culbert. "Our entire operation is worth only a million dollars." The experiment, with heavy emphasis on wire copy, was tried for a year and a half, then abandoned. Culbert now calls the paper a "hybrid, somewhere between a local and a metro," but its heart is really the heart of a local. "The entire strength of our paper is in its local news coverage," said Culbert. "The fact that the Oakland *Tribune* does not do the job it used to do in covering Berkeley makes it possible for this paper to operate. We would go under now as a metro-wire paper; why anyone would read the *Gazette* alone for all his news, I don't know."

A Good Second Newspaper?

Unlike the San Mateo *Times,* the *Gazette* now hopes primarily to be a good second newspaper. Culbert's motto: "A local name in the paper is another paper sold." News of international importance is often underplayed in favor of local news; Culbert admitted that if he has enough good local news, "we leave out the wire stuff entirely." The paper shed one of its wire services—AP. This was not because Culbert preferred UPI, but because he felt the paper needed only one service and the AP contract ran out before that with UPI.

Given its proclivity for local news, the *Gazette*'s position at the bottom—along with the Vallejo *Times-Herald*—in coverage of six national news items was not unexpected (see App. III). But Culbert's news judgment for the frequently cluttered front page was confusing. The paper customarily ran a lengthy boxed story above the logo. There Culbert placed a story on the Knox Commission's regional government proposal (see p. 131), a better piece than a few of the larger papers carried. On January 13, 1969 he ran an excellent interview with Berkeley vice mayor Wilmont Sweeney, first Black member of the city council. The interesting and informative story was punctuated with seven candid photos of Sweeney in a masterful job of layout.

In the very same edition, however, the *Gazette* showed its concern with sensation, drugs and crime. The headline of the first lead was "Bizarre Drug 'Guinea Pig' Case Here," and the second lead had "Police Identify Man Slain in Berkeley." When in late December 1968, Red China exploded a minor nuclear device, the *Gazette* placed the story in the page one box over the logo. By way of comparison, the San Jose *News,* San Mateo *Times,* and Oakland *Tribune* placed the story on page two; the *Examiner, Chronicle,* and *Mercury* on page one below the fold; the Palo Alto *Times* and Vallejo morning *Times-Herald* did not carry it at all. On January 18 the *Gazette* gave the lead spot to a $3,500 bank robbery, rather than to the University of California Regents' meeting in Berkeley.

Although editor Culbert claimed a rapport with the Berkeley Black community, the paper supported the attempts of a parents' association to recall three members of the Berkeley Board of Education who supported integration of the public schools. Despite some recent improvement, the paper has not properly covered the Berkeley integration struggle.

Nor was it insignificant that two unsuccessful attempts have been made to challenge the *Gazette* and speak for the majority of the community. The Berkeley *Review* (which lasted about one year) and the Berkeley *Citizen* (which lasted about three) were not underground papers. The *Freedom News* is still publishing monthly in opposition to Owens' other paper, the Richmond *Independent,* which has dealt shabbily with the Richmond Black community and has done nothing about Standard Oil pollution in that city. The two Owens papers are like peas in a pod.

Editorial and Feature Pages

The *Gazette* editorial and feature pages merit mixed reviews. J. R. "Kacy" Ward's "What in the World" column is a gossipy link to the old Berkeley community to which the *Gazette* appeals. Culbert, who, for an editor, does a great deal of writing and reporting, contributes a daily column in which he regularly says more about happenings in Berkeley than writers in the *Mercury, Tribune,* or *Chronicle* say about their respective cities unexciting syndicated columnists include Holmes Alexander, Max Lerner, Bruce Biossat, Allen and Goldsmith, and Don MacLean. The *Gazette* usually ran only one unsigned editorial each day, however, and would profit from another one or two. Along with the *Chronicle* (and the Palo Alto *Times*) the paper was a Bay Area leader in space devoted to readers' letters. But too much space was given to such entertainment features as "Berry's World," handwriting expert Paul Farrar, crossword puzzles and horoscope news.

Summing Up

Clearly the *Gazette* is not a paper suited to a university community like Berkeley. About the best that can be said for it is that, unlike the San Mateo *Times,* the *Gazette* is at least willing to discuss some of the problems in the community, regardless of its own position. In the present era of indistinguishable small papers, this is no small accomplishment. But the *Gazette* is a long way from being a force in the community. At most, it is an anachronism, speaking for a Berkeley that has long since passed. It is not powerful enough to affect the flow of events in any direction.

VALLEJO (MORNING) TIMES-HERALD (28,534)

Until mid-February, 1970, former State Senator Luther Gibson had one of the most tightly controlled newspaper monopolies in the Bay Area, in his ownership of the Vallejo morning *Times-Herald* and the afternoon *News-Chronicle.* Unlike the situation in San Jose, where the subscriber could take either or both of the Ridder papers, the Gibson publications were dual circulation: you could not get one without the other. This served to keep neighboring papers out of Vallejo.

On February 18, however, the afternoon paper was cut back from a daily to a weekly, appearing on Wednesday only. Oddly enough one of the big factors behind the decision was that Vallejo newsboys could not be counted on to deliver two papers. Said managing editor Wyman Riley,

> We had a monumental circulation problem. The kids just didn't seem to care. We had a turnover of a different carrier every six months; we were getting into some of the poverty kids as carriers, and often money collected was just taken home. Pretty soon our bonding company wouldn't bond the carriers anymore. We would have needed two separate circulation systems.

Costs of newsprint and labor also played a part. Although no editorial personnel were cut back, the dismissal of composing room workers led to a rocky period in February and March during which the remaining shop workers showed their displeasure by missing deadlines, losing type, misplacing page proofs and dropping lines from stories. "We had a hell of a time of it," said Riley.

Focus on Local News

While the 28- to 40-page weekly focuses exclusively on local news, or national news with a local angle, the morning *Times-Herald* tries to take up the slack. A women's section and feature page opposite the editorial page have been added from the old *News-Chronicle,* increasing the daily by four pages. Half the comics between the two papers have been dropped. "Space is a real problem now," Riley said. "We have to edit more tightly, but we still have a news hole of from 90 to 100 columns."

The papers maintain a four-man bureau in Fairfield, the county seat, and two-man bureaus in Vacaville and Napa. San Francisco and Sacramento are left to the wire services, a circumstance with which Riley is rather unhappy. In an effort to improve the paper's offerings from these areas, Riley scans the *Chronicle, Examiner, Tribune, Bee* and others for articles of regional interest. He then either deletes the bylines and runs them, or puts the information in his own daily column, which appears on the editorial page. Although the propriety of this practice is questionable, Riley is probably more aware than most other Bay Area news executives of what the competition is doing.

To Riley's credit, local news had a prominent place in the *Times-Herald.* The front page generally maintained a balance between local and national stories, and the editorial page frequently dealt with local issues. (See pp. 132–135 for the papers' campaign against regional government.) Once a week the entire editorial page was devoted to readers' letters. Although the Gibson philosophy committed the paper to a complete news package, national and international news offerings were as weak as those in the Berkeley *Gazette,* which is admittedly a local paper, and is not meant as a substitute for the *Chronicle* or *Tribune.* Appendix III shows the *Times-Herald* at the bottom, along with the *Gazette,* in its coverage of presidential stories, the cold war, the Presidio "mutiny" trial, the mid-east crisis, congressional news and Vietnam. Nor was the *Times-Herald's* record on continuity any better than the *Gazette's.* Stories on the above-mentioned continuing events were not run every day, nor did they generally appear in the front parts of the paper.

Mixed Views on Performance

Of all the news executives interviewed by the authors, Riley expressed the most satisfaction with the performance of his papers. He maintained that they have taken the lead in almost every worthwhile community project and that they have been a factor in the city's freedom from any major racial trouble. One former journalist, now a resident in Vallejo, did not agree. She said,

> From reading the local papers, you would never guess that Vallejo has a large and uneasy Black population, that our schools are severely racially unbalanced, that many school buildings are totally inadequate and the program is not meeting the needs of the children. I could cite other instances, but instead I'll say that generally the paper [*Times-Herald*] adopts a head-in-the-sand policy and seems to see only good in Vallejo.

With the energies of the staff no longer split between two papers, Vallejoans may soon be receiving a better morning paper. Riley is eager for editorial expansion. With the demise of the *News-Chronicle,* the afternoon San Francisco *Examiner* and the Oakland *Tribune* have an opportunity to make inroads in Vallejo, and perhaps force improvements in the *Times-Herald*.

PALO ALTO TIMES (44,684)

The reputation of the *Times* was found to be quite high among Bay Area publishers and press observers. It is viewed as one of the area's best local papers: well edited, involved and serving its community.

In bulk and appearance the *Times* was indeed impressive. It offered at least 40 to 50 pages daily, and occasionally approached 80 pages on Wednesday and Saturday. Its front page presented a good balance between local and wire stories, and the layout was often imaginative. Occasionally there was a tendency toward too much black type in the headlines, so that the eye did not know where to rest, but the news judgment was generally solid. There was an occasional wild headline, but sensationalism was kept to a minimum, except for student violence stories, particularly at Stanford.

The local papers in the Bay Area's two leading university towns, Berkeley and Palo Alto, are both politically conservative. Editor Alexander Bodi sets the tone at the *Times*. "People may not agree with me," he said, "but at least I'm honest about my feelings." Like Mike Culbert at the Berkeley *Gazette,* Bodi was most upset by student demonstrators. He was especially exercised over Students for a Democratic Society (SDS) and an ever-changing and expanding group of "subversive" activities, which Bodi has christened "communistic-fascistic." A group of

Senator Eugene McCarthy's supporters picketed the *Times* during the pre-election period in 1968 because they felt the paper was not giving fair treatment to the Senator. Bodi called the picket line a communistic-fascistic pressure device.

Although the paper dealt with troubles at San Francisco State and Berkeley with a good deal more restraint than most Bay Area papers, the advent of trouble at Stanford brought forth a different treatment. The sit-in at the Applied Electronics Lab and the April Third Movement roughly coincided with the appearance of a street sale edition of the *Times,* which carried a *Chronicle*-like banner to attract customers. Stanford radicals were frequently the subject of this banner, which emphasized their activities and statements. Nothing has so angered the student community in Palo Alto as Bodi's insistence on printing the addresses of radical groups—this during a wave of terrorist bombings engineered by rightwingers in San Mateo County. It should be noted that the *Times* was critical of the underground Los Angeles *Free Press* when the latter printed the names of narcotics agents in the state. The editor also recommended that a radical research group be hounded out of existence by city officials.

The paper has developed a relationship, although belated and tenuous, with the Black community in East Palo Alto. Bodi showed his pride in running a daily syndicated comic strip with a Black youngster as one of the main characters, and he has talked about starting an internship program for aspiring Black journalists. The paper frequently runs feature stories on Black self-help projects, and on concerned Black citizens who are working in the community. The editorial page has also shown an awareness of Black problems. Perhaps more indicative of the *Times*'s concern, however, is the fact that subscription delivery service in the ghetto was sporadic until the Black weekly *Peninsula Bulletin* was started as very weak competition. *Times* service then showed a marked improvement.

Specialty Writing and the Editorial Page

In addition to a healthy supply of wire copy—much broader national and international coverage than was offered by the neighboring San Mateo *Times*—Bodi could also be proud of his imaginative speciality writing. The "Family Leisure" section presented excellent material on food, fashions and home furnishing. Joyce Passetti and Carolyn Snyder do informative work in these areas. Dave Wik's sports pages give detailed coverage to Stanford athletics and local high school activities. In Dick O'Connor the *Times* has a perceptive sportswriter who is not afraid to print stories of team mismanagement and intrigue, as he did concerning the 1969 Oakland Athletics, Manager Hank Bauer and owner Charles Finley. One of his pieces on team dissension was pirated by the *Chronicle, Examiner* and *Tribune*. Arts editor Paul Emerson runs the best entertainment pages of any local paper in the Bay Area. Emerson hires outside talent for film, drama and music reviews; the result is a page more literate than any but those of the two San Francisco dailies.

Editor Bodi is justifiably proud of his editorial page. Most of the local editorials are written by thoughtful Ward Winslow. And the *Times* opens its columns to letter-writers on a more generous basis than any other Bay Area paper. Bodi also writes frequent columns on both local and national subjects. The editorial page of December 23, 1968, not untypical, offered a column on a state college trustee's view of Black demands; a piece by Bodi describing a speech by Saul Alinsky at the Commonwealth Club; and an unsigned editorial on the air pollution problem caused by the Kaiser-Permanente plant in Los Altos. Bodi has instituted a regular feature known as "Around the Beats" which allows staff reporters to write interpretive pieces about subjects they cover. It is undoubtedly a good outlet for the reporters' desire to analyze in print, and it gives a needed dimension to the news. Other papers could well emulate this feature. A comparison of the Palo Alto *Times*'s editorial and feature pages with those of the San Mateo *Times* makes the former's good quality even more apparent.

A Too-Small Staff

The chief problem at the *Times* seems to be that its able staff is much too small. Time after time, the Northern Santa Clara County Bureau of the San Jose *Mercury-News* covered events that were not touched by the *Times* in its home territory. And there were periods when issue after issue of the *Times* was disappointing to those who prefer depth coverage to five-inch stories. Nonetheless, the *Times* often offers something for every member of the family who is outside the activist orbit. And the local activists, especially those at Stanford, often seem to read the *Times* to get angry.

Santa Rosa Press-Democrat (47,228)
Regional Coverage

The 1970 census may show that the Santa Rosa *Press-Democrat* is one of the few newspapers in the country with greater circulation than the population of the city in which it is located. The *Press-Democrat* naturally sees itself as a regional newspaper, serving readers in Lake, Sonoma, Mendocino and Marin counties. It offers three editions: one for northern Sonoma and Lake counties; a second for southern Sonoma County and the Petaluma area; and a third for Santa Rosa.

To cover the territory the *Press-Democrat* has full-time bureau men in Ukiah and Petaluma, plus part-time stringers in Fort Bragg, Willits, Lakeport, Healdsburg, Sebastopol and other small towns.[3] Major afternoon competition comes from the San Rafael *Independent-Journal,* which has been making inroads in southern Sonoma County circulation, and from small dailies in Petaluma and Ukiah. Neither the San Francisco *Examiner* nor the Oakland *Tribune* represents much of a threat to the *Press-Democrat.* The local staff has remained at 25 or so over the past few years, with no plans in the offing to enlarge it.

The paper is owned by Mrs. E. L. Finley, widow of the publisher who was a leading Democrat and postmaster. If the paper doesn't step on many toes nowadays, it may be because Mrs. Finley has been friendly with Establishment people over a number of years. A rather more pointed complaint came from one critic who noted that the *Press-Democrat* did not publish at all on Saturday, and that a good part of the Monday and Tuesday papers was evidently prepared on the preceding Friday and Saturday.

Given its setting in the Redwood Empire, the paper has devoted much attention to environmental affairs, covering coastal access problems caused by the Sea Ranch development, redwood logging and PG & E's attempt to build an atomic power plant in the area. Managing editor Art Volkerts described the *Press-Democrat*'s editorial philosophy on such questions as being generally "in favor of industry and users." Although the *Press-Democrat* supported the atomic power plant, Volkerts claimed the paper's thorough coverage of the controversy played an important part in its defeat.

A Sedate Newspaper

Also as a reflection of its idyllic setting, the *Press-Democrat* was the least strident, emotional, or sensational paper of those surveyed. The front page showed an equal emphasis on local-state news and national-international, although lead stories were frequently of a local nature. It relied wholly on UPI and Copley Press Service for non-local material, which limited the amount of depth and background information presented.

Although approximately equal in circulation to the Palo Alto *Times,* the *Press-Democrat* trailed in its coverage of the arts, family life and

---

[3] Stringer: one who is employed by a newspaper to report on activities in his local area. He is retained either on a fixed monthly salary (usually no more than $100) or is paid on a piecework basis for everything that appears in print.

fashion. The editorial page was also disappointing. It offered no local writer and confined local criticism to the one unsigned piece each day. These editorials were, however, much superior to those in the San Mateo *Times*. Jack Anderson, W. S. White, Victor Riesel and some UPI columns provided the usual opinion fare. The letters to the editor space was generous, but some of the filler—such as "Bygone Days," "Grin and Bear It," "Almanac," and the "Country Parson"—could be sacrificed to make room for some local editorial comment.

Two major problems in the next few years will be: keeping pace with the expected population growth in the northern counties, and giving the growing Mexican-American community a voice in the paper. For now, the *Press-Democrat* impresses as a responsible, sedate reflection of community sentiment, at least a part of it.

The Six Sunday Papers: Distinction or Dullness?

The circulation of Sunday papers is traditionally higher than that of dailies, indicating that many subscribers expect a little extra on Sunday—enough to allow some of them to skip the rest of the week's offerings. Many editors in the Bay Area viewed the Sunday paper as a repository for material that did not fit during the week, and as a chance to "catch up with events" and put them in perspective.

The nine-county area has six Sunday papers. In terms of circulation, one is large, two are medium-sized and three, small. The field is straddled by the Sunday *Examiner and Chronicle,* the giant hybrid resulting from the merger in 1965. The Sunday Oakland *Tribune* and the San Jose *Mercury-News* are a distant second and third, followed by the much smaller Santa Rosa *Press-Democrat,* Hayward *Review,* and Vallejo *Times-Herald.* (Although the Contra Costa *Times and Green Sheet* has a Sunday edition, it is not geared to publishing a special Sunday package. Consequently it has been excluded from this study, which covered the period between December 23, 1968 and March 4, 1969.)

Certainly the most notable characteristic of the Sundays in the study was their lack of personality or distinctive "feel." The similarities in organization, space allocation, use of local talent and special sections were obvious. Sunday magazines could be switched from paper to paper, and few readers would be aware of the substitution. The arts and entertainment in the Bay Area were, with one exception, covered with the same depth and sophistication as in Cleveland or Detroit, where offerings are perhaps one-quarter as rich. Only infrequently did a column or section shout "I am uniquely of this paper," as do the Sunday Los Angeles *Times*'s *West* magazine, the New York *Times*'s "News of the Week in Review," and the Sunday St. Louis *Post-Dispatch* editorial page.

Serving a combined readership of 1.2 million households and offering from 80 to 220 pages, the Sundays seemed to be healthy, although their uniformity and lack of distinction suggested that the readership may be held through force of habit.

The Giant Hybrid

SUNDAY SAN FRANCISCO EXAMINER AND CHRONICLE (640,004)

This Sunday combination is not a united effort of the two staffs, but rather a morning *Examiner* to which the *Chronicle* has chipped in a Sunday magazine, editorial section and comic pages. Only the cheerful face and column of William Randolph Hearst, Jr. (Editor-in-Chief of the Hearst Newspapers), always appearing on page one below the fold, distinguished the Sunday *Examiner*'s news section from those of the rest of the week. Usually filling 32 pages, the front news section was a bit longer than the weekday section. A few more wire service interpretive pieces, such as one on Mayor Lindsay's problems in New York or Italian economic troubles, found their way into print. But there was nothing consistent about the Sunday news philosophy, and often during the period under study the front section was slim in news value.

The *Examiner* editorial page, with the exception of the Hearst column, was identical with weekdays: local writers Dick Nolan and Guy Wright, syndicated Sydney J. Harris and Hearst reporter Bob Considine and two or three unsigned editorials. The *Examiner*'s capable music and drama critics, Alexander Fried and Stanley Eichelbaum, were compressed into two small columns of a two-page "Lively Arts" section, a maddeningly slender Sunday obeisance to the arts. Dwight Newton on TV, Dorothy Manners with gossip, a few more pages of news, and a short section for the hobbyists customarily completed the editorial-feature section.

The Sunday Travel section, edited by Georgia Hesse, is easily the best such section in the Bay Area, with much locally written material, helpful advice on preparing for trips and excellent travel suggestions. The women's section started strong, with a profile on a female San Francisco doer, but ended in a pile of gossip columnists from Suzy Knickerbocker to Harriet van Horne. The greatest disappointment among *Examiner* contributions is the *California Living* magazine, a 40-page, full-color excuse for advertising with little redeeming social or literary value. It housed no more than three "major" articles, each including a page or two of text and accompanying pictures. Subjects were almost exclusively lightweight; political stories were avoided, and rarely was a San Francisco problem discussed, and then not in detail. *California Living*, unfortunately, is the model (and best of the lot) for all but one of the locally produced Sunday magazines. There seems to be no effort to move in the direction of *West* magazine at the Los Angeles *Times*. *West* has been focusing on articles of broader appeal, with an emphasis on travel and California politics. The quality of writing and depth of research in *West*'s articles far exceeds those in *California Living*.

The challenger to *West* is part of the *Chronicle*'s contribution to the Sunday paper: *This World* magazine. Editor Richard Demorest has chosen a news magazine format to review the week's news events. Because he does not have even one-hundredth the staff of *Time* or *Newsweek*, the review is essentially a pastiche of rewritten wire service ma-

terials assembled under standing heads. Some lengthier articles from
the New York Times and Times-Post services were often placed at the
rear of the magazine, but *This World*'s redeeming features comprise the
most literate music and art criticism in any of the Bay Area Sundays. A
typical array would include a major serious music piece by Robert
Commanday; records reviews and a shorter piece by Heuwell Tircuit;
Ralph Gleason on jazz; a generous book section edited by William
Hogan; and Alfred Frankenstein writing on art. These would combine for an interesting and distinctive 20 pages. Harold Gilliam, one
of the Bay Area's ablest conservation writers, appears every other week
in *This World*.

The pink, pull-out center section of the magazine, entitled "Date
Book," is another matter. Draped around movie, theater and reducing
ads in 1969 were the "columns" on film and stage stars, one cut above
the Earl Wilson variety, mostly wire service puffs for movies about
to be released or starlets on the way up. The week's television listings
were surrounded by a panoply of cheesecake photographs with soph-
omoric captions. Were it not for a valuable "On the Town" section
listing, in tabular form, the coming events in music, art, sports, night
clubs and restaurants, the pink section would be an insult to *Chronicle*
readers.

"Sunday Punch," the *Chronicle* editorial and feature page edited by
Carl Nolte, is among the most praiseworthy of single Sunday sections
because it is distinctly the *Chronicle*'s: it has personality, it is challenging and it is fun. The handling of this section makes one wish
that the Sunday *Examiner and Chronicle* were under the *Chronicle*
editors' direction, just to see what they would do with it. Local
columnists Herb Caen and Art Hoppe, sports editor Art Rosenbaum,
traveling essayist Stanton Delaplane, Count Marco and others all contribute to "Sunday Punch." Also appearing fairly regularly in 1969 were
the New York *Times*'s James Reston and Russell Baker, TRB of the
New Republic, Stanford's Nobel prizewinner Joshua Lederberg and
various other features from the *Chronicle*'s wealth of syndicated material. Add a generous helping of pictures and zany reports from Scott
Newhall's far-flung foreign stringers, and you have a section of interest,
if not cohesiveness.

In sum, the Sunday *Examiner and Chronicle* was hardly juicy enough
to curl up with for more than an hour or two. It was clear that the men
behind it are aware of the type of material that succeeds in major Sunday papers (such as a weekly news review, travel, opinion, magazine-type
pieces, art and theater criticism). But they have not invested enough
energy in the Sunday combination to make it much more appealing

than an overstuffed weekday edition. A Sunday magazine with some real punch, more analysis and feature material, and an enlarged news section are prime goals to guide needed improvement. But this may be too much to expect from a shotgun marriage.

Two Papers of Medium-Range Circulation

SUNDAY SAN JOSE MERCURY-NEWS (187,924)

The fruits of the *Mercury-News*'s emphasis on ad linage and promotion were most evident in the combined Sunday creation from the two Ridder papers: a massive paper, frequently over 200 pages. In California, it is second only to the Los Angeles *Times* in bulk. The cornerstone of the paper was a substantial news offering (over 40 pages) filling the first three sections. Although the same weakness in local news reporting that afflicts the daily *Mercury* and *News* was also evident on Sundays, national and international stories were well covered by material from AP, UPI, New York Times, Times-Post and Copley news services. Many lengthy pieces that were not time bound found their way into Sunday *Mercury* and *News* columns: Duvalier and Haiti; ministates causing U.N. headaches; how model schools in Portland aid poor children; American youth revolution at the crossroads. A weekly "Sacramento Scene" column from Lou Cannon was another valuable addition to the news pages before he moved on to Washington.

The *Mercury-News* shows the greatest individuality (and potential) with "Focus," a combination news review-editorial-travel-book section. Its outstanding feature is a front page devoted to depth study of a single topic: heart transplants, man's genius for fouling his own planet, a revolution in military education and the like. Some of the material came from wire services, often supplemented with related local articles by *Mercury-News* staffers. The single-page news review seems a more sensible approach (given staff limitations) than the *Chronicle's* effort. The editorial page featured different columnists each week, including Wicker and Baker of the New York *Times,* Bill Henry and John Averill of the Los Angeles *Times,* and William Buckley and James Kilpatrick. One lively column is "The Mercury—1869" in which Daniel K. Stern of the promotion department offers excerpts from the paper 100 years ago. Careful editing of such material can produce columns that throw more light on unfolding events than do articles by many contemporary political pundits.

Travel pages at the end of "Focus" were well done, although they offered less than those in the *Examiner-Chronicle.* Real estate, which either headed its own section or formed part of another, was largely puffery received from construction and building materials firms. The

"Today's Women" section was traditional, with heavy emphasis on fashion, beauty hints and bridal announcements.

One *Mercury-News* Sunday problem is the poor quality of magazines. Two of them, *California Today* and *Entertainment Calendar*, are locally produced. *Parade* circulates nationally, but with declining popularity. Trying to please everybody, it engages no one. *California Today* is not much better, with unexciting filler on pets or decorating, and homemaker and gardening columns that seemed to avoid discussion of serious questions. *Entertainment Calendar* presented music, drama, and film criticism of a quality far below the *Examiner and Chronicle* level. Much of the 20-page section was devoted to a TV pullout, gossip columns and Hollywood notes.

The *Mercury-News* would do well to concentrate its energies on one magazine, incorporating and expanding the best of the arts criticism and gardening-homemaking articles, and adding desperately needed material on San Jose problems. Nowhere in the more than 200 pages were local concerns discussed intelligently on a regular basis during the period of our study. This kind of focus on local matters will be essential if the Sunday *Mercury-News* is to become a San Jose newspaper and develop its own personality. At present, only its bulk and the embryonic "Focus" section separate it from run-of-the-mill American Sunday papers.

SUNDAY OAKLAND TRIBUNE (237,417)

With less than half the pages of the Sunday *Mercury-News,* the *Tribune* makes up for its lack of size—and consequent dearth of national and international news—with the best local writing in the Sunday market. Stories on San Francisco Bay fill and on regional air, water and transportation problems have become Sunday fixtures at the *Tribune.* Breaking either on the front page, or on the first page of the second "Metropolitan News Section," such stories often run to 40 or 50 inches, plus pictures. For example, conservation expert Fred Garretson wrote a series entitled "Our Polluted Bay," which included articles on industry and Bay pollution, and on the San Francisco sewer plan.

The *Tribune* has also used the "Metropolitan News Section" effectively in presenting complex information on overlapping regional government jurisdictions, and in explaining what various regional commissions do. Other local stories such as the Knolls Center speech therapy program in Richmond, and little theater in the East Bay, have also been highlighted.

The total Sunday news offering was typically a rather thin 24 to 30 pages, and the editorial "News and Comment" section was the poorest of the three major Sundays. Ed Salzman provides a sharp column on Sacramento politics, but the syndicated material was less stimulating than *Chronicle* or *Mercury-News* offerings. There was no attempt at a week's news review.

In its magazine lineup the *Tribune* offers *Parade;* an unabashed home improvement tabloid entitled *California;* and *Entertainment Week.* As for entertainment, it is significant that the *Tribune* has the manpower to break away from the stereotyped movie and TV celebrity articles that dominate most such magazines (including the *Mercury-News's*), but has chosen not to do it. Music critic John Rockwell and art critic Miriam Dungan Cross were usually restricted to one page each (often less), and the book review section was a bit over a page. All were jammed unceremoniously into the rear of the magazine without being highlighted with cover displays, as is so often the case with *Chronicle* arts pieces. The *Tribune* could markedly improve its magazine by giving greater space, freedom and control to its own arts writers.

The editorial and entertainment sections of the Sunday *Tribune* could stand hearty infusions of the same imagination that goes into the "Metropolitan News Section." It is disappointing that such valuable local news coverage is offset by a pedestrian editorial and opinion section, and a dull, functional entertainment page. Even without the *Mercury-News's* bulk or the *Examiner and Chronicle's* riches of syndicated material, the *Tribune* is gamely competing in the Sunday field. But many of its best players may be on the bench.

◇ ◇ ◇

Although no one Sunday paper was clearly satisfying on all counts, an amalgam of elements of the three major Sundays analyzed above would produce an interesting newspaper. Add to the *Mercury-News's* bulk and national and international coverage the *Tribune's* local coverage, the *Examiner's* travel section, the *Chronicle's* "Sunday Punch" and emphasis on art, music, dance and drama, and some publisher would be well on his way to a superior Sunday paper. He could take his pick of available sports sections (all competent), women's pages and comics. The *Chronicle's* "Peanuts" would be essential. But for today's reader, buying all three at a newsstand cost of $1.05 (35¢ each) and wading through a combined total of 400 pages of newsprint is too high a price to pay for one decent Sunday newspaper.

Three Papers of Smaller Circulation

SUNDAY SANTA ROSA PRESS-DEMOCRAT (49,133)

The *Press-Democrat* made a few concessions to the idea of a Sunday paper, one of which showed much initiative. Each 50- to 60-page

Sunday edition included an "Empire Living" section, (with the first page devoted entirely to some subject of interest to residents of the northern counties). Staffer Bob Wells, who writes most of these lengthy features, has presented everything from shipbuilding at Mare Island and agricultural research at U. C. Davis to a driving guide through four Redwood Empire counties and a tour of the little Sonoma County town of Shellville. Wells writes clearly; the pictures were interesting and the topics never dull. The *Press-Democrat* can be proud of these Sunday pieces.

The rest of the Sunday fare, however, was mediocre. In each issue there was a single editorial page, with syndicated columns from Anderson, Buchwald, Lawrence and Hoffer. There were no major news features, background stories or news reviews. The arts were jammed together on a single page that encompassed dance, music, books and radio. The familiar Sunday magazine, *Medley*, is a bit more ambitious than its counterparts in Oakland and San Jose, although its goals are even less clearly defined. It seems to be both a news magazine and a do-it-yourself supplement, and the two approaches do not mesh well: *Medley* included fix-it columns, comics, travel notes, a feature or two from various news services, a TV pullout, fashion, decorating ideas and hobby columns. Naturally, in 16 pages (excluding the comics and TV listings), nothing was done with much depth. The nationally circulating *Family Weekly* supplements *Medley*.

Given its staff size and circulation, the *Press-Democrat* provided the minimum for a Sunday, with a bit of a bonus in Bob Wells's work. But at least the paper is more closely identified with the needs of the Redwood Empire country than is the *Mercury-News* with the needs of San Jose.

SUNDAY VALLEJO TIMES-HERALD (28,714)

The *Times-Herald* made the fewest gestures toward a Sunday edition of any of the Bay papers. It offered no special Sunday magazine other than the syndicated *Family Weekly*, and the single editorial-feature page was equivalent to the weekday page. Such topics as travel, the arts and entertainment, farming and ranching, which could merit an entire section, must fight for space each week.

Every Sunday the paper ran above the logo a front-page boxed story with a Vallejo angle. Some were locally written, while others came from news services. Hospital openings and other civic projects were favorite material, although such subjects as sensitivity training and pay increases for local federal workers have also been studied.

Of most interest on Sunday are three columns, two of them syndicated. Jenkin Lloyd Jones, a Tulsa newspaper editor, contributes one; Henry C. MacArthur writes another from Sacramento. Dugald Gillies, formerly an aide to publisher Luther Gibson when Gibson was in the State Senate, does a Sunday piece on Vallejo problems. Gillies, described as a "freelancer" by a *Times-Herald* staffer, is associated with the California Real Estate Association, and writes from that perspective.

The "Social Panorama" section included food and gardening news, along with the brides, and there was usually a single page for auto and travel news. Sports coverage was strong, as in all the Sunday papers under study.

Of comparable size to the Sunday *Press-Democrat,* the *Times-Herald* has nothing to match the "Empire Living" feature or even the *Medley* magazine. In contrast, a bit more effort in Santa Rosa has produced a better Sunday paper.

SUNDAY HAYWARD REVIEW (37,977)

With 80 to 90 pages, the Sunday *Review* is the largest of this group. Some of the extra space was devoted to local news, spread throughout the news sections. The *Review* also tended to run more AP and UPI feature and background material than did the Santa Rosa or Vallejo papers; wire copy usually filled the pages at the back of the sports and women's sections.

Previewer magazine consists mainly of television listings, with a few puzzles for the kids, and a one-page "Calendar of Fine Arts" showing events in the East Bay. *Family Weekly* completes the magazine package.

The editorial and feature pages presented more syndicated columnists—including Goldwater, Hoffer, W. S. White and Childs—than the other small Sunday papers, but there was little local innovation in this part of the paper. A "Career Corner," focusing on a different career each week, was an interesting *Review* feature. A single arts page and a puff-filled real estate section were dull.

In sum, the similarities of the three small Sundays overwhelmed the relatively minor differences that enable a reader to distinguish among them.

◇　◇　◇

The importance of having good Sunday papers can be seen from the viewpoints of both the editor and reader. Many editors feel that the Sunday paper is a convenient place for much background and wrap-up reporting that is crowded out of the weekday editions. The comparatively higher Sunday circulation figures indicate that some Bay Area readers rely on the Sunday editions to perform this catch-up function. A good Sunday paper must, therefore, include a news section large enough to accommodate feature and background material, and some sort of news-in-review section. This latter might concentrate on a local news review for the previous week, since *Time* and *Newsweek* provide good national and international reviews.

One reason people spend more time with the Sunday paper than with weekday editions is the entertainment value of the Sunday offering. The comics, a magazine section, arts pages, a travel section and other specialties contribute to this entertainment package. A good Sunday paper should offer some of these entertainment and leisure specialties, concentrating on local travel and outing ideas, house and garden hints, and the local film/theater/music scene. These are some basic requirements for a Sunday paper that would be worth several hours of its readers' attention, once a week.

Papers Published Weekly, Monthly or Occasionally

In several studies of the weekly press, Professor Alex Edelstein and his associates at the University of Washington have categorized the editors of weekly newspapers in two groups, the "community-oriented" and the "journalist-oriented." If an editor is community-oriented, he will seek consensus and may gloss over even the major faults of his community to promote what he considers to be the greater good. If an editor is journalist-oriented, he will stress conflict, printing all the facts he can gather, although they may present to the community an image that many readers would prefer not to see.

This classification represents much more than an academic exercise. An editor who was told of Edelstein's conclusions said, "Sure, when the local sheriff dies, the journalist editor thinks there was foul play and tries to investigate. The community editor tries to see something positive even in this. He wants to write, 'There's a pretty new widow in town.'" Most newspapermen will agree that many of the men who run weekly newspapers tend to fall into either the community-oriented or journalist-oriented categories. They may doubt, however, that the division is quite as neat as the typology suggests.

Emphasis: Cooperation or Conflict?

Thus, it is certain the most community-oriented editor will, on occasion, print news that reveals community flaws. Conversely, the journalist-oriented editor, however dedicated he may be to disclosure, almost automatically presents many columns of news and features that promote the community's betterment and image in a way the Chamber of Commerce would approve. It may be, too, that the vast majority of weekly newspaper editors shift between community orientation and journalist orientation, depending upon the issue, the personalities involved and the circumstances. Almost any number of variables may be at work, including the editor's mood and temper on a particular day.

Neat or not, these categories are useful. For it is axiomatic that some editors stress cooperation rather than conflict, and that others stress conflict rather than cooperation. Such distinctions are useful in weighing the worth of a newspaper.

Edelstein's concepts are valuable in another way. They enable us to look at local weeklies and evaluate them against the image of an ideal: a mix of community and journalist orientations. Local progress is a satisfactory goal for any newspaper, but it is usually better served by disclosing unfortunate facts than by hiding them. On the other hand, the editor who is so sensitive to his role as an adversary that he publicly casts suspicion on nearly every action of local leaders—the crusty editor who sets himself up as the conscience of his community—may injure the community more cruelly than the editor who is in the pocket of the Chamber of Commerce. The great trick is to balance the roles by serving at once as the voice of the community's pride and the conscience of its shames and concerns. In the words of an editor of the respected Sonoma *Index-Tribune,* it is necessary to "prod and praise with equal fervor." No duty in journalism is more difficult.

As one veteran of weekly journalism pointed out,

> The problem of balancing roles is more difficult because it's hard to carry on hit-and-run journalism in a small community; you have to live with those whom you report. In a city you might expose a misfeasor and have him replaced. In a small community, he may be the best available, bad as he is. In many small towns, the citizens are happier with a mediocre physician than none at all.

The task of the small newspaper is even more difficult because of its peculiar financial problems. Many big advertisers and advertising agencies ignore weeklies. This means that the publishers of weeklies, in the words of one of them,

> must depend for 60 to 80 percent of their revenue on supermarkets. It takes 1,000 homes to support a market. The owner wants those 1,000 covered, plus another 2,000 in a concentric circle. He doesn't give a damn what else is in the paper so long as it's "safe." He just wants a copy of his ad at those homes by Wednesday afternoon. Hence the fact that virtually all successful conventional weeklies have a shopper. Papers without this kind of geographic coverage and without the market ads, have a hell of a financial problem.

Steve McNamara of the *Pacific Sun* offered a cogent explanation for the increasing number of small newspapers. He said,

> They have cropped up because there has been a need for them. *But:* it is highly important that one recognize the technological side of this. Without cold type composition and web offset printing in central plants, these papers couldn't exist. And that is a development of only the past 10 or 15 years.

Moreover, McNamara predicted,

> Smaller papers are going to be very strong in this country. It is now a nation of participants, rather than spectators. Hearst used to provide social scandals, axe murders and other vicarious thrills; TV does that now. And anyway, people are more involved in participating in their own environment. It is technically impossible for a metro to serve these small spheres of influence. The secret is finding a coherent interest group that

can provide the needed revenue either through advertising or, very occasionally, through circulation alone. Ten years from now it will all seem so simple. Right now it's rough. . . . But then if those of us who are doing it now waited for 10 years, it would all be done!

The Weeklies

The weekly press in the Bay Area presented a lively picture, with 96 newspapers in the field. They offered a significant potential for the area, and a major problem in evaluation. We tried a three-point approach in selecting and judging some of the best weekly papers. First, we began by reading a great many weeklies. Second, we asked a highly regarded editor-publisher to list those that seemed to him to be "complete" in the sense of balancing community and journalistic orientations. Finally, we wrote to the editors of every Bay Area newspaper and asked them to nominate the weekly they considered best.

Each of these methods has flaws and shortcomings. Our reading of the weekly press was not complete. We were further handicapped by lack of knowledge about the communities in which each of these papers was published. In addition, we knew that the editor-publisher's judgments might be colored by the kind of newspaper he himself produced. Finally, the editors' nominations were limited by the fact that no one could read all the papers regularly. Most of the respondents restricted their nominations to weeklies in their own counties, rather than choosing among the many published throughout the Bay Area. The ethnic papers, the religious papers, and the papers published less often than weekly thus had much less chance of being considered in such estimates than did the conventional weeklies.

Nevertheless, there was a striking similarity between the list provided by the single editor-publisher and the list based on nominations of the Bay Area editors who responded to our letters. Our own reading (primarily during December 23, 1968 and March 4, 1969) of the weeklies that were nominated, caused us to agree substantially with both lists.

NOMINATED AS "COMPLETE NEWSPAPERS" (Listed alphabetically)

The editor-publisher listed these as "complete newspapers":
Burlingame *Advance-Star* (twice a week)
Cupertino *Courier*
Livermore *Independent*
Milpitas *Post*
Novato *Advance*
Pacific Sun
San Jose *Sun*
Sonoma *Index-Tribune*

NOMINATED FOR "HIGH QUALITY"

On a second level of "high quality" newspapers, the editor-publisher listed:

Los Altos *Town Crier*
Oakland *Montclarion*
Pacifica *Tribune*
San Francisco *Progress*
Terra Linda *News*

NOMINATED AS "BEST"

Most of these selections were echoed in the editors' nominations. Those nominated as "best" by two or more editors include:

Berkeley *Post*
Burlingame *Advance-Star*
Cupertino *Courier*
Los Altos *Town Crier*
Milpitas *Post*
Novato *Advance*
Oakland *Montclarion*
Pacific Sun
Pacifica *Tribune*
San Bruno *Herald*
San Francisco *Bay Guardian*[1]
San Francisco *Monitor*[1]
Sonoma *Index-Tribune*

It is easy to understand why these papers were listed, considered "complete," or nominated as "best," especially when compared with such routine weeklies as the Menlo-Atherton *Recorder,* the Morgan Hill *Times,* and the Los Altos *News.* The routine papers sometimes seemed to avoid anything more controversial than a dogfight, and their reporting and editing were uninspired. The papers listed here, on the other hand, not only challenged local Establishments on occasion, but they also displayed a degree of specialization in reporting that enabled them to speak with authority.

When reading quality weeklies, we sometimes wondered why they are so often only way stations for reporters and editors who yearn for the world of the daily paper. The scope of the weekly is limited, and sometimes the pay of its employees is skimpy but the other compensations are great. To know a community, to be responsible for informing

---

[1] Inclusion of the *Monitor* and the *Bay Guardian* was a special tribute to those two papers, because they do not exactly fit this nomination category. The *Monitor* is a diocesan paper. The *Guardian* is a monthly.

it, to be able to alert most of the community to its own virtues and flaws —these are (or should be) excellent compensations. Certainly, some of the proprietors of the ambitious weeklies—Steve McNamara of the Pacific *Sun*, Mort Levine of the San Jose *Sun*papers and the Milpitas *Post,* and Robert Lynch of the Sonoma *Index-Tribune*—are among the many good weekly editors who seemed to be happy with their lot.

The excellence of some of the weeklies may be suggested by these items:

• The owner of the Pacifica *Tribune* once exposed shady business practices by pulling a wire loose from a television set, then sending it around to local shops for repair estimates. He did the same with a car. The stories reporting the wild estimates of the TV and car repairmen alerted his readers to a danger, and doubtless persuaded the repairmen that their estimates should have a nodding acquaintance with reality.

• In her column, "Your Dollar's Worth," in the February 12, 1969, Milpitas *Post,* Dr. Mabel Newcomer chided the San Jose *Mercury* for sloppy thinking, or worse, and warned readers:

> The answer of the "House Doctor" (whose column appears in the San Jose *Mercury*) to the woman who complained that her storm windows failed to meet the promises of the "fast-talking" salesman who had persuaded her to buy them was: "It is much better that way. Suppose salesmen told you the truth about the products or services they sell. Our economy would go into stagnation."
>
> The *Chronicle* also had published this column, omitting these introductory comments. And the business world as a whole surely would not subscribe to such a doctrine.
>
> The basic purpose of the Better Business Bureau is to protect the honest businessmen from the dishonest. But fraudulent business practices are still a common phenomenon, hard to reach in our mobile society.
>
> You are probably all familiar with the "special" offers of the sewing machine agencies that appear from time to time in this area.
>
> One of these, for Riccar machines, offers discounts on a $149 model ranging from $10 to $80, depending on the emblem noted in individual letters. The "lucky ones" get a free machine plus a four-day vacation for two in Las Vegas.
>
> There are conditions on this gift. You must call in person at the machine center (where you will probably be "switched" to a more expensive model). You must purchase a five-year prepaid Service and Instruction Policy at $12.95 a year ($64.75 total). And the "free" vacation specifies only free hotel accommodations and nightly champagne parties.
>
> I judge by the omissions that plane fare, meals, and other entertainment is at the expense of the lucky ones. An individual with firm sales resistance might save money by taking the specified model (if it ordinarily does sell for $149) and foregoing Las Vegas, but the Federal Trade Commission has cited the Riccar offer as a "bait and switch" fraud.

Dr. Newcomer went on with other matters that helped protect consumers in a forthright column of the sort that is difficult to find in the dailies.

· An editorial in the *Pacific Sun* is worth reprinting:

> Worried parents gather in Novato, demanding to know why the schools can't "do something" about the bizarre appearance and behavior of some students and teachers. In Mill Valley and Sausalito, some Tam [Tamalpais] High students get together and start their own school. They are dissatisfied with the kind of education they are getting.
>
> Behind these events lies one fact. Schools are becoming more and more like total life corporations and less like places where students go to get information with which to make their own decisions.
>
> Consider the functions which a school system performs: it runs the main in-county transportation system; it offers the principal recreation program; it has an enormous food service department, producing more meals than all the restaurants in the county combined; it runs the biggest driver-training school; it is hip-deep in the medical business, giving tests for sight, speech, hearing and psychological disorders; it is a vast "job placement" bureau; it is the main adult source of sex information; it lays down the Establishment line on drugs, and in some cases is supposed to rule on length of hair, skirts, and general physical appearance. In the time left over, it is supposed to lay on a bit of knowledge.
>
> Is it any wonder that school people become increasingly trapped in the administrative mentality? And is it any wonder that students become increasingly unhappy with the system?
>
> The blame cannot be assigned to the schools. Most school people, or at least most teachers, want mainly to teach. The blame must be assigned to the parents, who are madly loading their rightful responsibilities onto the school system.
>
> How long should your kid wear his hair? That is something for you to work out with your kid. Until you stop bringing the school system into it, your kid's chances for an education will be mediocre at best.

The foregoing discussion suggests that some significant gaps in Bay Area journalism are being filled in a few places by good weeklies. But other serious lapses require the two-fold remedy of better coverage by both dailies and weeklies throughout the area. Perhaps the weeklies' unique contribution lies in their potential—realized now and then— for providing an authentic community voice, fostering local leadership and encouraging a sense of community identity.

Published Monthly—More or Less

There is a spiritual kinship between the Bay Area weeklies—even the conventional ones—and the monthlies, because neither group is in the dominant position of the dailies. Beyond that, however, the kinship is distant. Many of the monthlies seemed to be published because their proprietors looked at the world around them, found it flawed, and decided that the flaws were caused by conspirators. There actually are a good many conspiracies, some of them criminal, others only the comfortable conspiracies that develop from easy agreements between selfish men: you help me get mine and I'll help you get yours. Consequently, there is plenty of meat for the conspiracy theorist's grinder.

Many of the theorists fail to recognize, however, that some of society's flaws are caused by accidents. Because they often do not distinguish between accidents and conspiracies, they know too many things that are not true. Yet in the end, the conspiracy theorists perform a valuable service. If the more conventional newspapers were not locked in the framework of national and local myths, not to mention their own self-interest, they would root out and publish the conspiracies. The theorists would then be left to make what they could of the accidents, and their newspapers would die swiftly. But the conventional newspapers, even the atypical *Chronicle,* ignore too many of the conspiracies and are involved in some of them. This provides both a role and a foothold for the maverick publishers.

This is far from a complete description of the reasons for the monthlies' existence, of course. Much of the fervor that goes into publishing some of the monthlies is rooted in causes that transcend particular controversies. Thus, although it is easy to imagine that there might be no *Bay Guardian* if the conventional press were more alert and devoted to the public interest, it is difficult to imagine that anything the conventional press might do would usurp the role and function of the *Freedom News* of Richmond.

It is not easy for the authors of this study to give suitable credit to unorthodox monthlies. We grew up in the tradition of so-called objective journalism as practiced by conventional newspapers. The tradition called for straightforward, dispassionate reporting, as nearly objective as fallible humans could make it. More recently, the tradition has made way for interpretive reporting: news stories that attempt to analyze, clarify, explain—but with as little of the personal opinion of the writer as can be managed. If we have sometimes wondered whether the old tradition or the relatively new one of interpretation is adequate, we have nonetheless been opposed to outright advocacy in the news columns.

The monthlies we are discussing, however, are nothing if they are not advocates. Sometimes in the news columns of the *Bay Guardian* and the *Freedom News,* the reporters were actually editorial writers. The fervor of their causes is a partial explanation. The fact that the papers are published so infrequently must provide another motive. When one has a cause, and can get at his readers only once a month, the pressure to promote a point of view must be overwhelming.

And so we were willing to consider these monthlies separately, as representative of many others that come and go in the Bay Area. We concentrated our reading during December 23, 1968–March 4, 1969, with some subsequent updating. We evaluated them in terms of what they attempted to accomplish, rather than judging them by standards that other kinds of newspapers seem to impose on all journalism. We bridled a bit at their outright advocacy; we doubted that these publications were as persuasive as they might be if they did not so often publish one point of view. At the same time, we accepted the premise that the conventional press is so overwhelming in its reach and power that extreme journalistic measures of this kind might be necessary.

BAY GUARDIAN

Bruce Brugmann's paper is so shrill, so laden with reports of alleged shady deals and under-the-table machinations, that a reader who is not a conspiracy theorist or a convinced Brugmannite tends almost automatically to reject much that his paper reports. But when one begins to look into the charges that fill the *Bay Guardian,* the reaction is quite different.

Is there really a contractual arrangement, as Brugmann reported, between the *Examiner-Chronicle* and San Francisco authorities whereby the papers can print legal notices in only a few thousand copies rather than all the copies of all editions? (This has enabled the papers to keep legal notices out of the hands of smaller publications.) Although it is consonant with city charter provisions, the arrangement appears to flout the public interest and may thwart taxpayers who want to read legal notices. The *Guardian's* account is accurate. *Examiner* executives admit it. (See fuller discussion on p. 45.)

Could it really be true that "Superchron" (Brugmann's name for the *Chronicle*-KRON-TV combination) set private investigators on the trail of Al Kihn, a former KRON cameraman? Kihn's complaints to the Federal Communications Commission about alleged shoddy KRON practices had delayed the station's license renewal, but such snooping is precisely what General Motors executives had done to Ralph Nader, the consumer affairs crusader, in 1966. Only two public apologies from James Roche, General Motors president, saved company officials from prosecution for intimidating a government witness. Surely, so soon after the General Motors fiasco, Superchron executives could not be so imprudent. But, yes, they were exactly that imprudent. They admitted it after prodding by the Federal Communications Commission.

Finally, was the overall voting record on conservation of State Senator Richard Dolwig of San Mateo County really as bad as a story in the

May 22, 1969, issue of the *Guardian* made it out to be? Could any state senator be as acquiescent to the lobbyists as the *Bay Guardian* made him seem? Dolwig's record seems to support the *Guardian's* thesis.[1]

It was not possible to check all of Brugmann's charges thoroughly. In some cases, only the principals in the individual controversies know whether the *Bay Guardian* is reporting them accurately. Did former Mayor John Shelley get out of the last San Francisco mayoralty race because he made a deal with his probable successor, Joseph Alioto? It is certain that Shelley declined to run, and that he now holds a plush position in Sacramento, arranged by Alioto. Brugmann charged conspiracy. But only Shelley and Alioto know for sure whether the allegations are true, and they deny them.

There were many other items, including allegations against the Pacific Gas and Electric Company, the Bay Area Rapid Transit District, and the Southern Pacific Railroad. Although the responses from the officials involved were often lame and unconvincing, we cannot know the full truth about these charges—at least not yet. What we do know is that a great many of the indictments that appeared in the *Bay Guardian* were quite true. There were enough of them to lead us to believe that Bruce Brugmann's paper is one of the most valuable in the Bay Area. Perhaps if more of those who come across copies of the *Guardian* were able to check its work and weigh its value, the paper might be able to add financial success to its journalistic accomplishments.

One reporter for a Bay Area daily commented:

> My own view is that the *Guardian* has drifted further left than it ought to go for good muckraking purposes and, further, that its makeup is too reminiscent of the old *People's World* or the *National Guardian* for its own good. But it performs a vital service just by being where it is and by being willing to print the stories that come its way. Thank God it's there.

Many a local journalist is convinced that the *Guardian* provides the most penetrating reportage in the Bay Area. There is some evidence, in fact, that it has penetrated too deeply. From 1967 through 1969, Brugmann's paper won four of the nine awards open to it in the San Francisco Press Club's "Pulitzer of the West" competition. In 1970, a Press Club committee decided that the only competitive category available to the *Guardian*, that for nondailies, would be open only to weeklies, thus excluding the *Guardian*, which is published monthly or less often. Investigating the action, Brugmann reported that the committee was headed by a public relations representative of the Pacific Gas and

---

[1] As indicated on p. 59, Senator Dolwig subsequently responded to intense pressure from conservationists and, in effect, reversed his position on the Bay fill issue.

Electric Company, and was made up almost exclusively of advertising and public relations men. Nearly all of them worked for companies that had suffered from *Guardian* exposés. This shabby incident caused two respected professors to resign from the panel of Press Club judges: Kenneth Stewart, Professor of Journalism, Emeritus, at the University of California, Berkeley, and Jerrold Werthimer, Professor of Journalism at San Francisco State College.

PLAIN RAPPER[2]

The reports on student unrest that appear in hundreds of newspapers and magazines must vie for attention with reports on Congress and the President, foreign relations, tax reform and more frivolous matters. These stories of unrest may do little more than persuade readers that there are pockets of turmoil in American society. In the more active periods, when one campus is inflamed, or when several are, the reports in the conventional press may suggest more—that youth is rebelling. But when a reader turns from the generality of the American press to publications like the *Plain Rapper,* it becomes quite clear to him that a revolution, or something very much like a revolution, is underway.

No one can judge how far this revolution will go, or even how many are committed to it. Certainly, the small circulation of the *Rapper* and similar papers indicates severe limits. Perhaps an end to the war in Vietnam will mark the end of the revolution. On the other hand, the militants argue that the war exposes fundamental flaws in American society, and that thoroughgoing change is essential.

At least for the time being, however, no one who reads the *Plain Rapper* can doubt its staff's commitment to revolution, which presumably also applies to an unknown number of readers. Labelled "A National Resistance Publication," edited and printed in Palo Alto, the *Rapper* published local and national stories on draft resistance and attendant aims. Consider this statement by 15 militants in Chicago, which was published in the fifth issue:

> Today, May 25th, 1969, we enter the Chicago Southside Draft Board complex at 63rd and Western to remove and burn Selective Service records. We still have a dream of being able to communicate with this society. But we can no longer confine our peacemaking efforts to the ordinary channels of polite discourse. For we are confronting an extremely urgent situation in which the twin evils of American militarism and racism are monstrously interconnected.
>
> The poor people of the earth are taught to hate and kill one another in order that the powerful can enjoy the freedom to increase their fortunes through exploitative foreign investments. At the same time, the expansion

---

[2] Not long after this section was written, the *Plain Rapper* died.

of war-related industries diverts tax dollars away from the social programs so desperately needed here. Born and raised in poverty and oppression, young men from America's urban ghettoes are forced to burn and kill poor peasants in a land of the Third World in order to preserve a "freedom" which they themselves do not even enjoy in their own land.

It is not by accident that we perform our act of creative destruction at the draft board center which menaces the South Side of Chicago. As white Americans, we bear a special responsibility with regard to the Selective Service System and the war machine it feeds; and we can no longer allow that system to function smoothly in our name, for we cannot tolerate the atrocities it perpetrates upon our brothers in America, in Vietnam, and in other parts of the world.

Our action is negative but also creative—for there is implied in our loud "No!" a quiet but hopeful "Yes!" in our elimination of part of the death-dealing and oppressive system, the prelude to the creation of life and freedom.

Having written their manifesto, the 15 (two of them women) broke into the complex, which housed more than 30 Chicago draft boards, stuffed 50 sacks full of files of draft notices, then dragged the sacks into the alley, doused them with gasoline and set fire to them. Instead of fleeing, the militants stood around the fire singing religious songs until they were arrested.

The same issue of the *Plain Rapper* carried many other reports of similar actions, and in tones that made clear the writers' leanings. An enclosed supplement on "The Imperial University" featured several articles that linked the campus with the military-industrial complex: a sketch of the military-university research complex, a report on capitalist involvement in the Third World suggesting that universities served corporate interests, an article showing how some of Stanford's activities were tied to firms in the nearby industrial park, a report on the Spring 1969 militancy at Stanford, and an article alleging that the Urban Coalition served the ends of business at home, just as U. S. diplomacy and the U. S. military served those same ends abroad.

Much of the issue was made up of investigative reporting. Many of the conclusions, however, rested heavily upon the convictions of the authors. For example, the report on the Urban Coalition stated:

> Two factors motivated these men to discuss urban problems. One was a simple desire to cool the explosive situation in America's ghettoes. Of equal importance was the desire to tap a potentially rich socio-economic market.

The latter point might be true, but the author's statement was the only evidence offered.

The *Plain Rapper* and similar papers often relied upon their readers' faith that what was being presented was gospel. Thus, they must usually be content with "convincing" only those who are already convinced.

Perhaps they can argue that spelling out self-evident truths would be like explaining why two plus two equals four.

In any event, the reader who wishes to learn the true depths of the outrage inflaming many of the nation's youth is not likely to understand either its depths or its dimensions unless he reads a paper like this one.

FREEDOM NEWS

If the *Plain Rapper* sometimes seemed to encompass every subject even remotely connected with the Vietnam war, it was single-minded compared with the *Freedom News*. Once known as the *Peace and Freedom News*—and once strongly linked to the Peace and Freedom Party—the paper apparently tries to cover everything in Alameda and Contra Costa counties that is ignored by the conservative Richmond *Independent* and Oakland *Tribune*. That gives it a wide range.

Almost entirely the product of Elizabeth and Meyer Segal, the *Freedom News* probably feels a kinship to those who write and edit the *Bay Guardian;* but the relationship is limited to sharing a broad liberal-radical doctrine. The *Freedom News* is more wildly varied than the other papers. The issue of April 1969, for example, began with a tribute to Martin Luther King on the anniversary of his death. Then came an attack on the Nixon Administration, a report on the activities of Women Strike for Peace, and a story on the troubles of Sam Warda, a bus driver charged with removing fallout shelter signs from public buildings. This much was predictable fare.

But the next page presented two long articles on pipeline bombings in the East Bay hills. Then came "A Special Education Supplement" that was something more than the title suggested: it was interspersed with stories on the Sierra Club, on an oil workers' strike and on half a dozen other subjects that seemed to have little to do with education. This was followed by other education stories and an unclassifiable variety: a short report on a Negro youth who was to represent the East Bay in the National Speech Championships, a speculative story on the successor to the district attorney, a minor item on a retiring San Francisco police lieutenant's advice to fellow officers ("Smile"), and long reports on local censorship and local elections.

The unity of much of this melange was purely negative: *Freedom News* readers couldn't get the material anywhere else—certainly not at the length the *News* presented it.

It is especially true that readers are not likely to see as many Black faces in other newspapers as appear in almost every issue of the *Freedom News*. There are white faces as well—perhaps more white than Black—

but the *News*'s coverage is clearly the Bay Area's most thoroughly integrated.

In the end, the value of the *Freedom News* springs from its emphasis on providing what other newspapers ignore. Where else can a reader find an "Air Pollution Award of the Month" with pictures of the first-place winners—the Albany dump and the Phillips Refinery at Avon—belching smoke into the region's air?

The Opinion Columns

There was a time, not so long ago, when the opinion columns in many a newspaper were as forthright as a kick in the teeth. "The trouble with the Baptists is that they aren't held under water long enough," alleged one editorial writer. Another commented: "Tallulah Bankhead barged down the Nile as Cleopatra last night—and sank."

Those who lament the opinion columns' loss of pungency can place the blame wherever they like across a wide spectrum of causes ranging from the disappearance of the frontier spirit to the departure of incisive newspapermen into novel writing and the theater. They may even blame the dead seriousness that afflicts some of the young journalists who, having been told that newspapering is no longer a game, but has become A Responsibility, reason that writing must be grimly humorless.

But the most accurate judgment may be the simplest: when a reporter becomes a columnist or an editorial writer, he is likely to settle at his desk and forget that reporting is the basis of most effective journalism. He merely thinks, mulling a clipping that represents someone else's work, then commenting upon it. He may weave neat phrases for a time, until the arrival of a deadline invites a platitude. But he is not likely to investigate first, then think and write. This is not true of every editorial writer or columnist, of course, but it is true of far too many.

In order to place Bay Area opinion writing in context, one should first look at the current habits of most American newspapers. During recent years, many publishers and editors have become concerned, if not nervous, about the monopoly power inherent in the single-newspaper-town situation. Accordingly, even their editorial pages have become less partisan. Some of those with liberal leanings are now careful to publish at least a few syndicated columnists who lean the other way. Some with conservative leanings seek liberal columnists. This lends a semblance of balance. But many editorial pages are still frankly partisan.[1]

The Question of Availability

Does the effort to balance syndicated columnists, right and left, please readers? Not all of them. The problem begins with defining terms.

[1] It is true that several distinguished newspapers—and many, like the Chicago *Tribune*, which do not deserve the adjective—have distinctively unbalanced editorial pages. The Arkansas *Gazette*, which is in many respects an excellent newspaper, publishes columnists whose political tone is remarkably like that of locally written editorials, in keeping with the desire of the publisher to instruct his readers in one stentorian voice. Although some of the New York *Times* columnists quarrel with each other in print on occasion, and the editorial writers are sometimes out of step with *Times* columnists, the editorial page is hardly balanced.

Doctrinaire liberals—especially those on the fringe of the radical move-
ments—doubt that there is a consistently liberal columnist outside the
underground newspapers. On the other hand, the devout conservative
who holds to the tenets expressed by Russell Kirk in *The Conservative
Mind* would probably doubt that American syndicates have offered a
consistently and devotedly conservative columnist since the late Westbrook Pegler was fired by Hearst. From such perspectives, there are no
syndicated columnists who can be used to balance an editorial page
because there is no one who can be placed at either end of the spectrum.

The problem of liberal-conservative balance is complicated by other
factors. An editor who decides on a policy of balance may find that
acceptable columnists are unavailable to him. Metropolitan papers
often buy up the right to publish syndicated columnists in their areas,
foreclosing publication by other metropolitan papers and smaller papers
in the same territory.

Thus, an editor may decide to balance a liberal like Jack Anderson
with a conservative like James Kilpatrick. He may then discover that
Anderson and Kilpatrick are either unavailable or too expensive. He
is able to buy and publish the column by Max Lerner, a liberal, and
David Lawrence, a conservative. So instead of publishing a digger like
Anderson and a cogent writer like Kilpatrick, the editor offers Lerner,
who is fuzzy and pretentious, and Lawrence, who probably has not hit
on a good idea for a generation.

Moreover, the editor who would like to publish James Reston's
column, or Russell Baker's, finds that he must buy the entire New York
Times News Service in order to get them. Any newspaper of consequence should use the Times News Service, but it is expensive, and
it is often monopolized by those territorial-rights contracts so dear to
metropolitan dailies.

The Voices of Dissent

Today, even an editor who avoids offering diverse opinions on the
editorial page is usually careful to open his letters-to-the-editor columns
to dissenting voices. If he actually provides an open forum in a substantial letters column, his own biases in editorials and column selection may not matter so much. Survey after survey has shown that letters
are among the most carefully read features of any newspaper.

Does this mean that a fair-minded editor allows anyone to write at
any length on any subject? No, it is obvious from many experiences
that extremists, kooks and those who thirst for personal publicity
flourish in such a setting—and offend other readers. The editor tries
to apply a rule of reason. (Unfortunately, a fairly popular rule among

some editors limits regular correspondents to one letter a month, no matter how sensibly and cogently they may write. This hardly seems reasonable when the editor propagates his own views every day.)

How does a newspaper play fair with those who oppose its policies? One distinguished editor said that he leans over backward all day long, mutters to himself that he is human and thus biased, and plays up letters from those who hold opposing views. The fair-minded editor also quells his itch to respond to the opinions of letter-writers. This does not mean that he never writes an editor's note in the letters column. Errors of fact must be corrected. If a correspondent argues that Senator Eugene McCarthy must be supported for the presidency in 1972 because McCarthy did so much to root Communists out of the State Department 20 years ago, the responsible editor must, in the public interest, note the difference between the late Senator Joseph McCarthy of Wisconsin and Senator Eugene McCarthy of Minnesota. But the editor should not respond in the letters column with a caustic note to a letter-writer who argues that Joe McCarthy purified the State Department. (Having studied McCarthyism, we doubt that the senator did much more than whip up hysteria against innocent people. But as editors considering such a letter, we would sigh and publish it.)

There is more to the philosophy of balance of opinion in many of today's newspapers, and some of it is unfortunate. Certainly, the growing reluctance on the part of editorial writers (or their superiors) to say much that is pointed makes many an editorial page increasingly useless. Some editorial writers argue, rather defensively, that they do not have all the answers, and that there is room on their pages for interpretation as well as advocacy. The point is well taken; interpretation and analysis are useful tools. Yet there is a strong suspicion that this statement is more often an excuse than an explanation. Certainly, it does not explain all the editorial salutes to Flag Day, Mother's Day and the Fourth of July. Perhaps this ought to be the rule of thumb: if an editorial writer has little or nothing to say, he should not write an editorial.

Few writers seem to be aware of the possible benefits of such a rule. In its absence one sees almost everywhere a mushy series of diffuse statements. So innocuous are most locally written editorial columns that the good ones—like those in the Washington *Post* and the St. Louis *Post-Dispatch*—are made to seem great.

With some notable and notorious exceptions, then, this is an opinion-writing era when most newspapermen believe that their freedom must be flavored with both responsibility and caution. It is not very exciting, especially if measured against an earlier era of personal journalism, when the editor and his most responsive critic might carry horsewhips. Only the underground newspapers, the new college dailies, and the radical sheets—and only a few of these—reach the level of passion and invective that characterized some of the old thunderers. We long for a more vivid note than most of the conventional newspapers strike today, although we suspect that journalism and the American people have probably gained something, even while losing color and pungency.

Where do Bay Area newspapers fit in this picture? To make a judgment, for nearly three months (roughly December 23, 1968–March 4, 1969) we read the editorial page, and the page opposite the editorial page, in each of the 10 newspapers sketched in pages 28–69: the San Francisco *Chronicle*, San Francisco *Examiner*, Oakland *Tribune*, San Jose *Mercury* and *News*, San Mateo *Times*, Berkeley *Gazette*, Vallejo *Times-Herald*, Palo Alto *Times*, and Santa Rosa *Press-Democrat*. Because some local columnists who write on general subjects are not published on either the editorial page or the op. ed. page (Herb Caen, for example) we read their columns as well. On the basis of our reading, we offer here some highly subjective judgments on letters-to-the-editor policy, columnists and editorial writers.

Letters to the Editor

We could judge certain aspects of these contributions in only a general way. Not being able to poll all those who have written letters to local newspapers, for example, we had no way of knowing how many and what kinds of letters have been rejected. We know that every Bay Area newspaper has published at least occasional letters fiercely opposed to the publisher's policy. All of the executives and journalists we interviewed maintained that they seek out opposing opinions. Undoubtedly, some letters that cut too close to the bone have been rejected. Frail humans will rationalize such actions with the easy explanation that another correspondent covered the same point, or the letter wasn't in good taste, or there was a possibility of libel—especially because at least one of these flaws is apparent in many of the letters that are received.

Some Bay Area newspapers refused to print letters supporting political candidates, on the ground that the supporters of many candidates would flood the letters column. These editors were, in effect, confessing their inability or unwillingness to select and publish the really good, the pointed and meaningful letters. In short, they were confessing their inability to edit—or their fear of the consequences of editing. Some local editors also refused to publish letters that quarreled with points of view expressed in editorials. They were thus unable to carry on a dialogue with their readers except by telephone, as they attempted to explain why certain letters cannot be published.

It seems axiomatic that such policies result in dull cut-and-dried material that is a poor excuse for a letters column. The editor who argues that opening the column to political advocacy will cause it to be inundated with letters should consider whether his paper rules out political advertising on the same ground. If it does not, he is in the peculiar position of allowing his readers a voice in local political matters only if they pay to be heard.

Some editors argued that a letters column open to correspondence supporting political candidates would enable shrewd politicians to organize letter-writing campaigns that would give them an undue advantage over their opponents. Again, however, an editor's job is to edit, and such an argument is a confession of his inability to do his job. Reflection might suggest, too, that candidates with insufficient funds for lavish billboard, television and newspaper advertising campaigns might be able to reach their constituents through the letters column, at little cost. It is doubtful that this would subvert democracy.

Nearly every Bay Area newspaper was guilty of publishing too few letters, and some papers also gave them little prominence. Our suggestion: let the editors study the readership surveys. These show that letters are far more widely and intensely read than editorials. Then let the editors attempt to justify the size of type, the headlines, the placement and the space given letters, compared with editorials. (This may be the clearest symptom of the inertia that afflicts much of journalism. Letters have always been published this way, so. . . .)

Daily Columnists

We could not assess in more than general terms the local-interest columns that could only be described as parochial pillars of tidbits. At their worst, they were riddled with the names of readers who only motored to Denver or Portland. At their best, they were made up of wry little ancedotes about local people and happenings. Because we did not live in each of the communities served by these columns, we were unable to assess their local value.

We can wonder about the style of most of them, which seems to be in Early Wisecrack. It is probably unfortunate for all the other anecdotal columnists that Herb Caen's style provided such a high standard for this kind of thing. But if none of the other columns came close to Caen's, few could be called as bad as the worst, which we judged to be Dallas Wood's "The Prowler" in the Palo Alto *Times*. It was filled with feeble anecdotage and trivia—items on a par with the fillers that tell how many ocean-going ships docked at Liverpool in 1965.

SAN FRANCISCO CHRONICLE

Assessing the *Chronicle*'s opinion offerings was a headache. The *Chronicle* presents the most provocative columnists among Bay Area dailies, including so many of them that it sometimes seems to be a "viewspaper." It is also overwhelmingly unbalanced; since the death of Lucius Beebe, who could write the most outrageously reactionary judgments in winning words, not a conservative voice is now to be heard unless one counts Joseph Alsop. Finally, the *Chronicle*'s huge package of columnists may add up to little more than a ton of feathers, a possibility of which we must take some account.

The leadership of the *Chronicle*'s columnists begins with Herb Caen and Art Hoppe. It is no more rewarding to try to define Caen's qualities than it is to try to dissect a joke, but certain values are clear. Unlike many another Bay Area columnist, Caen works. We do not know whether his work consists of sitting by the telephone and taking calls that pour in from public relations men and publicity-seekers (or having someone else take them), whether he picks up half his material from friends and makes up the other half, or whether he is the all-around-town boulevardier that his column makes him seem. The important matter is that we found his column regularly packed with pointed information and anecdotes. He sometimes filled it with one of those "essays" so dear to the columnist when he is straining for something to say that day, but ordinarily his prose poems to San Francisco came only on Sundays (he writes the Sunday column the preceding Tuesday) or when he was trying to catch his breath after a vacation.

No other Bay Area columnist is as deft as Caen. Most of his writing is lean. He has an unusually sensitive ear for the quip or the anecdote that is only marginally worth printing, and he apologizes for printing it with a deprecating phrase as effective as Johnny Carson's rueful and engaging recovery line, "That was a little bit of humor there."

Caen is much more than a gossip columnist, if only because the spread and intensity of his readership gives him unusual power. He may ride a political horse for only a sentence or two, but then another sentence appears on the same theme a few days later, and an anecdote a week later—and Herb Caen's political leanings become quite clear. They are distinctively liberal.

Beyond this, it is difficult to assess his appeal. It may be enough to say that every column, no matter how frothy the subject, suggested that an active intelligence had been at work. In the terms of what Caen produces—which is the only way to judge a journalist's work—he is an excellent writer.

Hoppe, who is less widely known than Art Buchwald and Russell Baker, may be the nation's best political satirist. Although Buchwald is better known, a genuinely funny man whose column misses as often as it hits, he seems bland compared to Hoppe. Russell Baker is probably the most gifted writer of the three, but he has trouble finding themes that will carry his wry commentary. Hoppe has more ideas, and richer ideas, than either of his rivals. It is easy to suspect, too, that Hoppe is much more the political animal than Buchwald or Baker. There is an acid quality in much of his political whimsy.

Until one tries to imitate it, Hoppe's method seems ridiculously simple. He observes the foibles of humans, especially those in government, focuses on one of their more dubious enterprises, and then imagines in print that it has been carried to its absurd conclusion. The result is political commentary of a very high order.

For all their great value, Caen and Hoppe are much more writers than reporters. Some of the specialized columnists do report and are fairly substantive. Ralph Gleason on pop culture, William Hogan on books, and Terrence O'Flaherty on television—often produce rich offerings. But Merla Zellerbach (Goerner), Stanton Delapane, Charles McCabe (an elegant stylist and a readable iconoclast), often write cleverly about very little. Count Marco writes offensively about women, and manages to offend men as well. Some issues of the *Chronicle* suggested that not a columnist left the building the day before; everything was spun off the top of somebody's head, and the reader seemed to be making his way over a mountain of whipped cream.

On Saturdays, most of the fluff writers appear to be resting. There is Lester Kinsolving, who is probably the only religion columnist a non-religionist can read both comfortably and profitably. L. M. Boyd and Milton Moskowitz pack their weekend syndicated columns with facts, a few of them valuable. Unfortunately, the Saturday *Chronicle* also carries an interminable column of puffery headed "After Nightfall." It is advertising in the guise of a column, and it is inexcusable.

The *Chronicle* reader arrives at Sunday with joy. The paper's chief contribution to the Sunday *Examiner and Chronicle* (known to some as "the Exonicle") is a section labeled "Sunday Punch." As noted earlier, it carries James Reston, Nicholas von Hoffman, "T.R.B." (a column from the *New Republic* that should lead some readers to that magazine) and others almost as good. A reader could spend as much time with the "Punch" section as with all the other Sunday sections put together.

In the absence of richer material in the locally written columns, the *Chronicle* should consider either publishing or releasing some of the syndicated columns it buys and sits on. Having contracted for the New York Times News Service, the management might consider publishing more often the perceptive work of Tom Wicker and C. L. Sulzberger. It might even consider giving full space to the columns it does publish. The list down the right side of the page opposite the editorial page— Hoppe, Jack Anderson then Abigail Van Buren—is hardly presented in complete form. Anderson's column and Abby's column usually are given much more space in other papers. If more space were needed, there is no known law requiring "Dennis the Menace" and "Bobby Sox" to appear opposite the editorial page. If a light attraction seemed essential, "Bobby Sox" might be moved, leaving "Dennis" to act as the barker who lures unsuspecting customers into the sideshow.

San Francisco Examiner

Much of the opinion writing in the *Examiner* is as old-fashioned as sarsaparilla. In one of his candid moments, the late Westbrook Pegler derided himself and all the other columnists of 30 years ago who thought they could, just offhand, deliver cosmic thoughts about absolutely anything. One usually despairs of trying to find the epitome— the example that actually stands for an entire class—but on Sunday, July 13, 1969, in his *Examiner* column, "Editor's Report," William Randolph Hearst, Jr., provided the clearest imaginable case to illustrate Pegler's point. Hearst's confession of ignorance was so striking that his exact words are worth savoring:

> Never before, to the best of my recollection, has this column been devoted to a discussion of economics and the mysterious but enormous role it plays in our national welfare.
> There are two excellent reasons for this:
> A—Economics was a subject I never studied in college.
> B—From what I have observed since then there are so many conflicting theories that only experts can pretend to understand them fully, and even then there is no general agreement, much less any semblance of unity of opinion.
> Just the same, inflation and the problem of controlling it have become so important that today I thought I'd put in my two-bits worth. And even though I am a non-expert in this non-science, most everybody else is in the same canoe.
> So here goes—a collection of thoughts, offered for what they may be worth, by one who was brought up to believe the essence of a sound fiscal policy is to be neither a borrower nor a lender.

Hearst then reported that he had become both a borrower and a lender, and continued on and on through a full double column of homilies. In essence, he was saying that he knew nothing about economics, that he was brought up to respect one kind of homely philosophy and practices another, and that, somehow, all this qualified him to instruct the 640,000 readers of the Sunday *Examiner and Chronicle.* What actually qualified him was his ownership of the *Examiner*—and that may lead some of us who are marginally intrigued by things the radicals are saying to wonder about the sanctity of property rights.

Not all of Hearst's columns were so distressing, and perhaps none of those written by the other *Examiner* columnists were. And yet threads of this kind of thing are found throughout the paper. Bob Considine, who has a choice position in the middle of the page opposite the editorial page, has long been a prize example of the glib reporter who covers sports and war and politics and space and international affairs—just anything that interests him—as though it were really possible to do all that meaningfully. The result is dismayingly superficial.

No doubt Guy Wright and Dick Nolan, the local columnists whose work appears on the page with Considine's, have many devoted followers. They are occasionally amusing and anger easily at injustice. Sometimes, though, the page dominated by Considine, Wright and Nolan featured its best offering in a column by Sidney Harris.

To the credit of the *Examiner,* the range of columnists on its editorial page was much greater than that in the *Chronicle* or in most of the other Bay Area papers. Carl Rowan is perceptive, if somewhat dull. William Buckley is still interesting. Max Lerner and Henry J. Taylor represent the syndicated extremes about as well as a tired old liberal and a tired old conservative can.

Often missing from this lineup was the very element the *Examiner* is in a good position to provide: hard-working, knowledgeable reporting about politics without regard for political ideology. This capability is represented by the team of Rowland Evans and Robert Novak, whose "Inside Report" is by far the best national political column that has surfaced in the last two decades. Evans and Novak may be wrong as often as most pundits, but they know how American government functions, especially party politics, and they work very hard.

Instead of sitting with a batch of clippings and their thoughts—a process that is indulged in by too many columnists ever since Walter Lippmann showed that a superior intelligence could make it pay—Evans and Novak make phone calls, wear out shoe leather, knock on doors, and talk to the people who are at or near the centers of power. The *Examiner* rewards them by publishing their column occasionally.

In sum, so much of what the *Examiner* offered was so much like what was offered years ago that it is tempting to wonder whether the paper is being edited for the emerging decade. Columnists are available who know what they are writing about, and who can write clearly and interestingly. The *Examiner* should publish more of them.

OAKLAND TRIBUNE

An almost certain sign that a newspaper avoids strong opinions—or fears offering them—is the frequent appearance of signed columns by Hal Boyle, Phil Newsom, and other wire service columnists. Boyle, an AP columnist, and Newsom, who writes for UPI, have much greater freedom than most wire service writers, and yet the wire service tradition of reporting—or, in any case, avoiding editorializing—flavors all their work. They may interpret and analyze (although Boyle seldom does), they may even venture a tentative opinion on infrequent occasion. But the thrust of strong advocacy is not in them.

There were other signs that the Oakland *Tribune* backs away from advocacy. Its local-interest columnist, Bill Fiset, is intent on amusing his readers, and does it very well. A great swatch of the page opposite the editorial page is given over to "Action Line," a service column for readers. Few of the other items that made their way to that page were any more challenging than Ann Landers, whose column is a fixture there.

Moreover, the few columns that did present a point of view were always preceded by an italicized Editor's Note: "The following views are those of the authors and are presented here to give readers a variety of viewpoints. The *Tribune*'s opinions are expressed only in editorials." This is not a general note standing for all syndicated columns, but is published over every syndicate offering.

Other journalists undoubtedly understand the reason for the *Tribune*'s policy, but many readers are ignorant of journalistic practice. They call to ask why the editor supports the views of Ann Landers, or President Nixon or even Al Capp. The editor explains patiently that he has done no more than print their opinions. "If you don't believe it, why print it?" comes the outraged rejoinder. There is some merit, then, in a slavish spelling out of the ground rules for publishing opinions.

But when this combines with the blandness of most of the *Tribune*'s offerings—and the kind of syndicated columnists the paper publishes— it causes a degree of wonder. The editorial page includes Roscoe and Geoffrey Drummond, grappling with national politics in their low-key way, Robert S. Allen and John Goldsmith reporting from the Right, and occasional columns by Flora Lewis, Henry Hazlitt, James Kilpatrick, and a clutch of little-known writers for Long Island *Newsday* and the Washington *Star*. Except for Kilpatrick, who gouges liberals fairly effectively at times, there was little that would seem likely to heat the blood of a loyal *Tribune* reader.

It was all a bit confusing. The late Joseph Knowland was said to run the *Tribune* with one hand and Alameda County with the other. His son William Knowland, the former U. S. Senator and present publisher, is reputed to have the same power, or something close to it. One would expect such strong individuals to produce a stronger paper.

SAN JOSE MERCURY AND NEWS

The San Jose papers could be considered together, and not only because they are under a single ownership. They are alike too, in an evident regard for balance of several kinds. This is not to say that they are identical twins. The *Mercury* editorial section was much more stable and interesting than that of the *News*, although it suffered from one of the *Chronicle*'s chief faults: the editors trimmed columns without regard to content. One critic pointed out:

> William Buckley, for instance, simply requires a larger compass than the *Mercury* usually allows him. He is invariably winding up to make a point when the column abruptly ends. I, for one, would prefer one full Buckley column to three half-Buckleys, largely because his style demands it.

There is political balance in the *Mercury* and *News*, with left-leaning Jack Anderson appearing in the *Mercury* (and at greater length than he is given in the *Chronicle*) not far from William Buckley's "On the Right." The *News* sometimes runs perceptive David Broder of the Washington *Post*, or a similarly liberal columnist, next to William S. White, a conservative. Art Buchwald's unclassifiable wit in the *News* is balanced by that of Russell Baker, equally unclassifiable, in the *Mercury*.

There is a kind of balance, too, in the generality of the editorial page and feature page offerings of the *Mercury* and *News*—the mix of outspoken columnists, and of those who interpret and analyze. Anderson and Buckley are examples of the first kind. Alfred Friendly of the Washington *Post* and the Roscoe and Geoffrey Drummond team stand for the interpretive variety. It was difficult to judge whether these papers carried more of one kind of columnist than of the other, especially because so few columnists appeared daily that the lineup was ever-changing. The *News*'s editorial pages, in fact, seemed to be constantly in flux. Certainly, however, the weight of the editorial sections of both papers leans away from advocacy, because of the frequent appearances of light offerings like "Barb," "Potomac Fever," "Inquiring Reporter," local-interest columns, and the advice column by Ann Landers. The *News* presented more of this than the *Mercury*.

Unfortunately, another kind of balance in the *News* is represented on the one hand by the incisive intelligence of a mind like David Broder's or Joseph Kraft's, and on the other by the infinite stupidity of the column headed "Dr. Crane." We presume that benighted areas exist where "Dr. Crane" could be an ornament to editorial sections. But for a newspaper in the Bay Area to feature his inanities—and guide readers to them with a line in the front-page index—is inexcusable. In a recent defense of television, Dr. Crane wrote:

> Television also helps reduce the divorce rate, as well as drunkenness and even highway fatalities! How?
> By keeping husbands at home, in front of the TV set.
> Otherwise, they'd roam to distant taverns to spend the evenings where immoral women often try to entice them and where their excessive use of liquor makes them a terrible hazard on the automobile highways.
> Remember, over 50 percent of auto deaths involve drinking drivers!

Responding to a reader named Eva who wrote to complain that her employer was consulting a psychoanalyst and urging the same treatment on his office staff, Dr. Crane wrote a column carrying these observations:

> Eva has "horse sense" or gumption.
> The basic aim of medicine is really to free humanity from the need to consult physicians.
> So the more you can learn to handle your own problems, the more money you can retain out of your pay checks! And the lower will be taxes!
> For medicare and the current mad stampede to hospitals, is zooming our tax rates dangerously high.
> Yet many people are such "Worry Warts" about their health that they squander literally BILLIONS every year on needless drugs, vitamins and medical consultation!
> Indeed, in Hollywood, it has now become a fad to have your own personal psychiatrist!

All in all, it would seem that the *Mercury* got the choice columns and the *News* got what's left. In ordinary cases of tight finances and unavailability of some columns, that might be an adequate excuse. But both the *Mercury* and the *News* can afford a better stable of columnists. A wide variety is available because they are apparently outside the territorial-rights zone of the *Chronicle* and the *Examiner*. The San Jose papers should do better.

SOME PROBLEMS IN SELECTING COLUMNS

The five metropolitan newspapers in the Bay Area have exclusive rights to a great many of the best syndicated columnists and understandably will not share their local columnists with smaller competitors.

Consequently there is not a great deal to be said about the columns in other dailies. There offerings are limited, in part, by restrictive contracts.

Most of the editors try to balance opinion columns to some extent by posing a leftist against a rightist, thus giving their readers a wider view of the world. Many of them selected the interpretive and analytical columnists, rather than those who fall heavily to one side or the other of the political spectrum. In the end, with only a limited number of columnists to present, this might be the better course. The lack of strong advocacy in columns written by some local editors and publishers suggested, however, that they might really have chosen this course because it was safer. All in all, when one considers how column selection is closely hedged in with restrictions, it is difficult to criticize the smaller Bay Area papers for what they present or fail to present.

The only remarkable aspect of local editors' column-selecting habits was their inability to recognize a superior column when it was offered. For example, two years ago Herbert Brucker, who for 19 years was editor of the editorial page of the Hartford *Courant,* began writing a column twice a week for the Palo Alto *Times.* Brucker is 70 years old, but nevertheless is the columnist who best understands what is happening among the country's youthful rebels. In column after column he has demonstrated unusual perception, without ever condoning the violence of the militants. Nor is his scope limited to the youth rebellion. Writing only twice a week, he felt constrained to say something meaningful in each column. The result was a collection of valuable insights presented in readable prose, a record that many widely syndicated columnists cannot match. But Brucker's excellent column—which is inexpensive and readily available—was published only by the Palo Alto *Times* and the Hartford *Courant.*

The obtuseness of the editors who ignore columns such as Brucker's is not really new. For years, when they have had the opportunity to buy the "Inside Report" of Rowland Evans and Robert Novak, many editors seem to have been yawning and buying Bruce Biossat, who, in turn, caused their readers to yawn. Seeking a conservative writer, they bypassed James Kilpatrick and purchased David Lawrence, whose column would be funny if he did not believe so devoutly in what he is saying.

Such habits are deplorable, although we may be oversimplifying a bit. Thus, it is granted, somewhat grudgingly, that our views may conflict with those of editors who, in trying to get the right columnists for the right space on the right days of the week, have encountered degrees of complexity not considered here. But commentators who believe that American journalism ought to rise to its best possibilities should express their opinions. In this instance, we are convinced that editors have a responsibility to overcome, as best they can, obstacles to the presentation of quality opinion columns.

Editorial Writers

If the columnists were difficult to evaluate because of their diversity, the editorial writers were much easier to judge because of their relative uniformity. No doubt they supported some excellent causes forcefully. Perhaps many agencies of government and praiseworthy civic enterprises were grateful for local editorials, and have reason to thank those who write them. Let us grant this value and its negative corollary: that some editorials have turned up irregularities and have put a stop to some undesirable practices. But when one attempts to evaluate the work of Bay Area editorial writers against high standards, the result is disappointing.

It is not that local papers failed to write intelligent editorials, or to offer interesting little commentaries on light subjects. Indeed, some editorials presented issue analyses and judgments that have been thought through carefully and expressed vigorously. For example, a long *Examiner* editorial on "The Malice Issue in Alioto Suit" clarified many of the issues incisively:

> Citizens absorbed in the continuing drama of *Look* Magazine v. Joseph Alioto, or vice versa, must surely find themselves confused by the direction and the vehemence of some of the moves made by the principals.
>
> For example it is unusual that Mayor Alioto should direct so much of his fire at Gov. Reagan. The Mayor charges that the Governor came into possession of an advance copy of the *Look* issue alleging Alioto-Mafia ties, and disseminated that copy to the news media four days before *Look's* distribution date.
>
> And it is extraordinary that *Look,* instead of standing quietly on its article, went before television with an elaborate rebuttal to Alioto's television reply to the article.
>
> The reason for most of these moves can be found in a 1964 landmark decision of the U. S. Supreme Court entitled Sullivan v. New York *Times.* The Court said the needs of democracy require that public officials must be subject to the broadest possible criticism. Because of this need, said the Court, a public official may not successfully sue for libel even though defamatory falsehoods are uttered against him—unless he can prove actual malice. The Court defined actual malice as the uttering of a defamatory statement knowing it to be false, or uttering it with reckless disregard for whether it is false.
>
> Mayor Alioto could prove that *Look's* charges against him were defamatory falsehoods—and still lose in court. He has to prove that *Look* knowingly and recklessly uttered defamatory falsehoods. That is his core problem, as lawyer Alioto knows and as *Look's* lawyers know.
>
> The Mayor might get his foot in the door on the malice if he could prove the *Look* article was transmitted deliberately for political reasons

along a certain channel: from *Look* to Reagan to the public. He is trying
very vigorously to do so. *Look,* responding with equal vigor, has denied
that it sent an advance copy to the Governor. Instead of a simple denial,
however, *Look* made a sweeping and comprehensive denial in lawyer
language.

. . . . .

The crucial malice aspect helps to explain the flurry of biting charges
and prompt replies on tangential matters like racial slurs, libels on the
City itself, inexperienced freelancers, etc.

More important, it goes far to explain why so much of the case is being
tried before the citizenry sitting at home in front of TV. This is the court
of public opinion, which to a public official is very often the highest of all
courts.

Probably we are witnessing, in the *Look*-Alioto moves, the emergence
of a natural pattern of conduct for cases where a public official is accused
and charges libel but must prove malice. As events of recent days have
shown, it is a pattern producing more of the "uninhibited, robust and
wide open" give-and-take that the Supreme Court sought to encourage.

Similar valuable editorials were found in other Bay Area papers: a
few in the Palo Alto *Times,* a few more in the San Rafael *Independent-
Journal,* at least one in every paper. Perhaps the *Chronicle* offered more
than any other local daily.

CRITERIA FOR JUDGING EDITORIALS

In judging editorials, we looked for consistent value. We looked for
grace of expression, clarity of writing, singularity of theme and purpose
and vigor of opinion. If an editorial advocates, it should do so unmistakably. If it explains or interprets or analyzes, the writer should present more than a reporter can in the news columns. If he does not,
why use editorial space that way?

Perhaps above all, we asked that editorial writers not waste their
time and ours by presenting an issue in the manner of a news story,
and then tacking on a short paragraph praising or vilifying the principal figure in the case. If the reader is swayed by a sentence or so of
flimsy judgment, he is persuaded for a very poor reason: because an
editorial writer says so. Such editorials are little better than salutes to
Flag Day: they fill space. Unfortunately, Bay Area newspapers featured
more of these than of the other kind, i.e. editorials presenting close
argument and thoughtful opinion.

There was also a curious absence of force and passion in most editorials. We do not believe that any considerable number of editorials
should be shrill, but it was possible to go for months without reading
a single editorial whose tone indicated unmistakably that the writer
really cared about what he was saying. Thus it was a pleasure to read

Scott Newhall's editorial reaction to a public Board of Education meeting in 1969 on the volatile issue of busing-integration. A number of citizens and a *Chronicle* photographer at the meeting were beaten by small groups of thugs opposed to the busing plan. The attackers escaped unidentified. Newhall's editorial called the men "self-appointed heirs of Hitler's brownshirts," "professional thugs" and "intellectually underprivileged . . . overnourished apes." He concluded with a challenge:

> The members of this band of social neanderthals are obviously too insecure and too frightened to come forward and identify themselves. But, if they miraculously should care to do so, they can either call GA 1-1111, extension 463, or come to this writer's office, which is Room 332 on the third floor.
>
> On the other hand, if this phantom squad of bullies cares to take umbrage at these remarks and wishes to continue its typical cowardly and disgraceful activities, it can catch the executive editor of this paper almost any week night on the darkened Fifth street sidewalk at the side entrance to the *Chronicle*. He leaves the building at approximately 8 p.m. each evening on his way home.
>
> Or, if they prefer, they can catch him quite alone in his San Francisco residence. The address is 1050 Northpoint Street. Simply ask the doorman for Apartment 708 and you will be escorted to the elevator.

We are far from suggesting that many editorials be written so pugnaciously. But it is refreshing on occasion to read an editorial that does not seem, like most of them, to have emerged from some institutional ooze.

WHY MANY EDITORIALS ARE INNOCUOUS

The cause of editorial innocuousness is quite clear. An editorial writer usually finds himself in the position of the public information officer in Vietnam who is not altogether certain how far he should go in telling the truth when briefing reporters on military events. Not quite knowing how much the general would say, he plays it safe and says very little. The general might actually be more candid—although he must also play it safe and say less than his immediate superior might say, and his superior must try to guess how much the President would say in similar circumstances—but the poor staff officer cannot be certain. This is the chief reason reporters would rather talk to generals than to staff officers, and in city hall to the mayor rather than to his press secretary, or in Washington to the President rather than to the presidential press secretary.

Like the staff officer, the editorial writer may be given full instructions, usually by the editor, before he goes to work. But the editor is probably not available at the moment of composition, when the writer is putting thoughts into words. Moreover, a publisher probably looms behind the editor, and perhaps a board of directors behind the publisher. They are not always threatening figures, but they can be.

Even when the system allows an editorial writer to submit his work for clearance, removing the ultimate responsibility from him, he is not really his own man doing his own work. But this is a far better system for most writers than having to write editorials and send them directly to the composing room for printing. Such a system is almost certain to produce a number of cautious editorials; the writer tries to imagine what the objections from on high might be.

Whatever the system, if two or three figures do not loom behind the writer, the newspaper as an Institution does. Such a presence inhibits some editors-in-chief, and may even affect publishers who write their own editorials. Who can really do his best work as the voice of an Institution?

These are all stifling influences, and they make some recent changes in European journalism quite understandable. There, a good many editors—as well as sub-editors and reporters—will work for a newspaper only if the management grants them absolute freedom. In effect, they have an agreement enabling them to write as they wish, at least for the life of the contract.

The malaise of editorial pages has other causes, some just as basic. For example, institutions change more slowly than individuals. Now that we are in a period of revolution, it is not surprising that newspapers are slower to catch up than some of the reporters and the syndicated columnists.

The newspapers and their editorial columns begin with a heavy handicap. The institutions of American society are under attack, and newspapers are substantial institutions. Not only that, other institutions look to them to lead in preserving the status quo. In such circumstances, it is not surprising that even the great newspapers have only a hazy and obscured vision of the future, during this period of unprecedented institutional challenge. They are understandably slow to admit the deep fissures of hypocrisy in American culture and rhetoric, and they are quick to focus on the clearly reprehensible tactics of the militants who are trying to effect changes.

THE CURIOUS CASE OF THREE PAPERS

We have noted a curious fact: the three Bay Area newspapers that are published in the home territory of the most active radicals—the San Francisco *Examiner* (San Francisco State College), the Berkeley *Gazette* (University of California), and the Palo Alto *Times* (Stanford University), often demonstrated the least editorial understanding. Perhaps this was because they have seen the militants at their most active worst. On the other hand, they also have had the best opportunity to talk to the radicals, and to try to discover what is on their minds—as well as what is in their hands. By pursuing this course, the papers might be able to write informatively about interesting facts: even though demands 1, 3, 7, 9, and 15 are either impossible of accomplishment or patently undesirable, 2, 4, 5, 6, 8, and 10 through 14 are reasonable and go to the heart of real failures of the university. Campus administrators may admit that the militants are right on these points. The editorial writers might also reflect on the fact that, whatever view one takes of militant tactics—and our view is that most of their tactics are witless and counter-productive—they often succeed. It is at least possible that the successes of the militants are decidedly temporary. It may be that the coming backlash will produce an oppressive atmosphere. But meanwhile those whose mission it is to think in print should weigh a sober question: Does anyone seriously believe that the structure of universities will be the same five years hence as it was last year?

The editorial writers might even go from there and listen to radical charges against American society. They would be likely to discover much the same thing they would have discovered about radical claims and charges against universities; some of the demands are impossible or the charges absurd, but many also point to demonstrable flaws and failures.

Finally, the writers might explore the history of revolution. With such homework, they could introduce perplexed readers to some of the thinkers who have reflected on violence, as well as to some of the behavioral scientists and philosophers who are attempting to dissect it. The next step would be to explain why so few of the "good" students are rising in protest against the interruption of their education. (To oversimplify, the explanation is that so many relatively apathetic students sympathize with the major demands—while deploring both other demands and the tactics of their fellow students—that they cannot in conscience oppose a movement promising to correct basic injustices.)

Bay Area editorial writers thus have had ample opportunity to deal more informatively with violence and protest. Perhaps they have investigated, and either have made or have failed to make the discoveries that seem to us so obvious. In any event, the results of neither judgment appeared in their work—perhaps because of the constraints mentioned earlier.

The most notable fact is that local editorial writers are not taking advantage of excellent opportunities to learn more about a great many matters beyond the youth rebellion. Three universities—Stanford,

Northwestern and Harvard—offer journalists a paid opportunity to come to campus and study anything they like for periods of up to a year. Few local editorial writers even bother to apply, presumably either because they are not interested, or because their employers will not let them go. When Stanford offered a free five-day conference on the "Second American Revolution" in June 1969, with a series of excellent lectures by authorities both in and outside academic life, Bay Area editorial writers were not among the participants. Similarly, when Stanford recently embarked on a unique and distinguished one-day-a-month seminar dealing with the problems of California's largest and least understood minority group, Mexican-Americans, representatives of the press were conspicuous by their scarcity.

This lack of evidence that editorial writers are interested in improving their product tempts us to side with the critic who held that few of them are much more than "tired reporters." In fairness, some of the obstacles we have pointed out as looming in the path of effective editorial writing may simply be too formidable. But in closing we again look at the editorials in the Washington *Post* and in the St. Louis *Post-Dispatch*—and envy their regular readers.

Case Study: Student Unrest

In assessing the performance of a number of papers in one area it was essential to find an issue common to all, thus permitting comparison. In the Bay Area this meant finding an issue with salience in such widely separated communities as San Jose and Vallejo. Student unrest was such an issue. It proved to be the most significant local story from December 1968 through April 1969, when violence exploded on campuses in many parts of the Bay Area. The situation at San Francisco State College was considered so important that papers of all sizes in all nine counties carried daily stories on activities there, and nearly the same level of coverage was given to the Berkeley Third World Liberation Front troubles.[1] Stanford University, San Jose State College, College of San Mateo, Solano College (in Vallejo), and the various locals of the American Federation of Teachers were all confronted with student unrest in the period studied.

While it was trying for police, politicans and reporters, this widespread activism was a press critic's dream. Over an 18-week period, from December 1968 through April 1969, the authors made content analyses of 10 Bay Area newspapers (see App. IV B for the choice of papers) to determine the quality of Bay Area press coverage. Extensive interviews were conducted with editors and reporters involved in the stories. The study also presented an opportunity to weigh the charges from all sides that the press was either being used by, or was catering to, students, politicans or administrators.

Although Paul Conroy, managing editor of the San Jose News, preferred to interpret criticisms from both sides as an indication of objective reporting, this was clearly wishful thinking. It has long been a comfortable philosophy in journalism that being hit from both sides indicates that the paper is playing it just right: straight down the middle. But it is also possible that being hit from both sides means that the reporting is so bad that everyone is outraged. The nation's press labored mightily to cover the difficult issue of unrest, and Bay Area papers have borne more than their share of such assignments. The press has heavy responsibilities, because it is often the only means of communication between dissident groups; along with television, it is the most important information source for the general public. As the nation's press corps most experienced in covering student unrest, Bay Area journalists should have some lessons to teach.

---

[1] The TWLF was the name given to a loose coalition of Blacks, Chicanos and other minority groups.

111

Dimensions of the Story

The single most important aspect of the student demonstration story was its longevity: 15 weeks of constant activity at San Francisco State; an equal period of sporadic activity at U. C. Berkeley and San Jose State; a two-week uprising at College of San Mateo. Bay Area papers plunged in and gave this story more space—much of it on the front pages—than any other issue, either local or national. *Chronicle* reporter Dale Champion has said, "Our file on San Francisco State

TABLE 3

STUDENT UNREST: COLUMN INCHES IN SIX BAY AREA DAILIES[2]
FEBRUARY 17–MARCH 4, 1969

Paper	Column Inches	
	Total	Ave. per Day
Berkeley *Gazette*	1667	119.1
San Francisco *Chronicle*	1531	109.4
Oakland *Tribune*	1419	101.4
San Francisco *Examiner*	1387	99.1
San Jose *Mercury*	871	62.2
Vallejo *Times-Herald*	683	48.0

[2] To make the content analyses more manageable in the time at our disposal, we selected from the 10 Bay Area dailies the big four (omitting the San Jose *News*), and added the Berkeley *Gazette* and the Vallejo *Times-Herald* for the sake of comparison.

looks like the file for World War II." Thus, a second aspect of the student unrest story was its sheer bulk, as measured in column inches published.

Table 3 presents the total number of inches six Bay Area dailies devoted to student stories. The period under study extended from February 17 to March 4, 1969, a time when San Francisco State, U. C. Berkeley, and San Jose State were all experiencing trouble. The totals included pictures and headlines.

Tables 4 and 5 give the column inches devoted to the Vietnam war (Saigon, Washington and Paris datelines) and the Pueblo investigation during the same time period. Figures from the New York *Times* are included for comparison.

Thus, during the period included in the sample, it was also possible to see the ratio between space devoted by the six Bay Area papers to student unrest and to the Vietnam war. The *Gazette* gave heaviest preponderance to the student story: 8.5 (student) to 1 (Vietnam). Next came the *Chronicle* with 4.5 to 1; the Vallejo *Times-Herald* with 3.9 to 1; the *Examiner* with a little over 3.1 to 1; and the Oakland *Tribune* with nearly 2.5 to 1. Last was the *Mercury* with 2.2 to 1.

The Pueblo investigation was a story of national importance carried by newspapers all across the country. This is the way the six Bay Area dailies allocated their space in comparison with the news play of the New York *Times* and with each other.

TABLE 4

VIETNAM WAR: COLUMN INCHES IN SIX BAY AREA DAILIES
AND THE NEW YORK TIMES
FEBRUARY 17–MARCH 4, 1969

| Paper | Column Inches | |
	Total	Ave. per Day
New York *Times*	916	65.5
Oakland *Tribune*	570	40.7
San Francisco *Examiner*	439	31.4
San Jose *Mercury*	402	28.7
San Francisco *Chronicle*	388	24.1
Berkeley *Gazette*	194	13.9
Vallejo *Times-Herald*	171	12.2

TABLE 5

PUEBLO INVESTIGATION: COLUMN INCHES IN SIX BAY AREA DAILIES
AND THE NEW YORK TIMES
FEBRUARY 17–MARCH 4, 1969

| Paper | Column Inches | |
	Total	Ave. per Day
New York *Times*	427	30.5
San Jose *Mercury*	285	20.3
Vallejo *Times-Herald*	277	19.8
San Francisco *Examiner*	175	12.5
Oakland *Tribune*	143	10.2
San Francisco *Chronicle*	110	7.8
Berkeley *Gazette*	68	4.8

Some of the variance in space allocation is attributable to differences between morning and afternoon papers. Also the student demonstrations were local, while the Vietnam and Pueblo stories were available by wire service only. Nevertheless, there is no question that the Bay Area papers devoted an extraordinary amount of space to the student protest story. In addition, the *Chronicle, Examiner, Tribune* and *Gazette* carried at least one front-page student story every day during the two-week period. The *Mercury* also carried a page one story every day for 10 days; and the *Times-Herald* carried stories 13 of the 14 days, 11 times on page one. Neither Vietnam nor the Pueblo investigation received such treatment. Even President Nixon's trip to Europe, which came during this period, was given less space than the student demonstrations.

Despite the massive, day-to-day coverage, the papers had a difficult time presenting the daily events in a context that made sense of the whole. This is the most difficult aspect of reporting a continuing story, whether it is a war, a strike, a trial or a demonstration. This problem was exacerbated by the large number of groups speaking to the public and contending for power, from Governor Reagan and the State College Trustees, to President Hayakawa of San Francisco State College and the many student organizations.

Issues Left Unresolved

The difficulty of providing continuity in complex and rapidly changing situations was exemplified by the fact that many issues were left unresolved in the newspaper articles from one day to the next. During the period February 3 to 7, 1969 (chosen at random) the *Chronicle* left 12 separate issues unresolved: on February 3, for example, President Hayakawa said he would reinstate striking teachers if they returned to classes on February 17, when the new semester was to begin. On February 4 the striking teachers said they would respond to Hayakawa on February 6. On February 5 the *Chronicle* reported that it was unclear whether teachers would obey a new restraining order to stop the strike, or even whether the order would be enforced. On the 7th Hayakawa informed the striking faculty who had lost their jobs that they would be rehired if they applied by February 10. Union president Gary Hawkins replied the union "probably would respond today."

And so it went with unresolved stories and events; deadlines, counterdeadlines, court dates, postponements, continuances and threatened demonstrations. The Oakland *Tribune* had eight such issues pending during the same time period for the Third World Liberation Front (TWLF) strike at Berkeley. The Berkeley *Gazette* had six. It is obvious that this caused confusion for readers, who were forced to juggle as many as a dozen events during a week or more, in order to keep things straight in only one of the strikes.

The problem was not so much that the papers did not try to fit all the pieces together—they did try—but the nature of the strike was not adaptable to the traditional demands of newspaper deadlines, pressures for new leads, and spot statements made in response to other spot statements. Most editors failed to realize that the reporting of every policy statement, demand and threat came to be counterproductive, because the reader was overwhelmed by meaningless detail. Probably not one Bay Area reader in a hundred could give even the barest outline of what happened month by month at San Francisco State. Said the *Chronicle's* Bill German, "I'm now leaning away from reporting all the nitty-gritty specifics of all the policy statements and meetings in an SFS-type crisis. . . . I want to present the bigger picture, the larger story . . ."

The "Bridge" Story and the "No News" Story

In an effort to establish continuity, papers have developed two kinds of stories. The first is a "bridge" story, designed to keep the reader up to date. Such stories are almost always from wire services. A UPI story appeared in the San Mateo *Times* on January 2. The head was "Classes at SFS Due to Resume Monday."

> Classes are scheduled to resume Monday at San Francisco State College —and militant student groups have vowed to resume a strike which has resulted in turmoil and violence on campus since Nov. 6.
> Leaders of the Third World Liberation Front and Black Students' Union have scheduled a strike rally Sunday night at Glide Memorial Methodist Church.
> Meanwhile, mediators Ronald Haughton and Samuel Jackson planned to meet today with representatives of the college, the American Federation of Teachers and State College Trustees.
> Members of Mayor Joseph Alioto's citizens' committee, formed to find a solution to the campus problems, also planned to meet today.
> The AFT is demanding improved working conditions, a bigger voice in administrative matters and granting of 15 demands made by the TWLF and BSU.
> The teachers' union, which represents about 300 of San Francisco State's 1,100 faculty members, has threatened to strike Monday if the issues are not resolved. The AFT also has urged teachers at the 15 other state colleges to join the strike.
> Formal opposition to the threatened AFT strike has come from the 115,000 member California State Employees' Association.
> Association President Robert Carlson, who charged the AFT was capitalizing upon campus unrest to "gain by force what it failed to gain by persuasion," said members of his group would not honor AFT picket lines.

Of what use is such an article? To those who have given even minimal attention to the strike it presented no new information, no new perspective. To those not familiar with the strike, it was much too rudimentary. Indeed, as an introduction it was positively dangerous: only an anti-AFT source was quoted; student demands were only hinted at; and there was no indication of what issues Haughton and Jackson were negotiating. It was a filler article designed to keep SFS in the news; this was hardly necessary in light of the hundreds of inches devoted to the story each week.

A Region's Press

The second type of story cloaks in a maze of unimportant information the fact that nothing happened on campus today. On December 28 the *Chronicle* ran a 30-inch piece headlined "The Crucial S. F. State Mediation Talks Begin." The key phrase came in the third paragraph: "... Ronald Haughton, the mediator ... *declined to comment* on the discussions." [emphasis supplied] That was the only real news in the piece. Seven paragraphs were devoted to who attended the meetings, plus the meetings of Mayor Alioto's citizens' committee; three paragraphs to a statement by Bishop Mark D. Hurley on what the committee hoped to do; and the remainder sketched strike background. Substantive articles on negotiations were rare. But articles about the arrangements for negotiations were many, and almost pointless.

TABLE 6

CAMPUS PROBLEMS AND THE U. C. REGENTS' MEETING:
COLUMN INCHES IN NINE BAY AREA DAILIES
January 18, 1969

Paper	Inches	Stories
San Francisco *Chronicle*	265	12
San Jose *News*	171	7
San Francisco *Examiner*	148	6
Oakland *Tribune*	124	8
Berkeley *Gazette*	123	7
Vallejo *Times-Herald*	111	8
San Jose *Mercury*	89	7
San Mateo *Times*	71	5
Palo Alto *Times*	25	3

Focus on Confrontation

Part of the blame for the inadequate strike coverage, despite the massive amount of copy, could be attributed to the news judgment of editors. All preferred to focus on confrontation rather than negotiation, and on headknocking rather than attitude changing. The greater the violence on campus—this was particularly true in San Jose and Berkeley—the more space the story was given. An excellent example of this news ethic occurred on January 17, 1969, when the U. C. Regents, including Governor Reagan, met at Berkeley to discuss University problems. Press stories noted that the Governor was jeered by students, a youngster made an obscene gesture at police, eggs were thrown at the Reagan limousine and glass was broken in University Hall. Incidentally, a number of important decisions were made at the Regents' meeting itself.

Table 6 shows that there was no lack of will or space to report the Regents' meeting at Berkeley. But what was the emphasis of this coverage?

Only the two San Francisco dailies put the disorderly incidents surrounding the meeting in the proper perspective. The *Chronicle* ran three stories: one 26-inch story on page one by Ron Moskowitz which described an important item on the agenda—the Regents' plan for overhauling the investment policies for the University's portfolio. On page eight another story of 17 inches appeared on the meeting; also on page eight Don Wegars covered the disorders in 18 inches. The *Examiner*'s education writer Lance Gilmore wrote a detailed, 63-inch, page one story on the meeting, placing particulars of the disorders in six paragraphs in the middle of the piece. Gilmore's excellent story was the best of the coverage.

The San Jose *Mercury* ran a first-page picture filling 28 column inches, showing demonstrators chasing the Reagan limousine with eggs. The story explaining the picture appeared on page 43 and was three and a quarter inches long! On results of the meeting, the *Mercury* presented 15 inches on page five from the Los Angeles Times-Washington Post News Service. The San Jose *News*, the Ridder afternoon paper having much circulation overlap with the *Mercury*, ran the same egg-throwing picture on page one with a 25-inch story combining both egg throwing and meeting results.

The Oakland *Tribune* ran a 12-inch, page one story under the head "Reagan Escapes UC Mob," accompanied by a 24-column-inch picture. The *Tribune*'s account of the meeting appeared on page three—13 inches long. Parts of the *Tribune*'s "mob" story were too dramatic to go unquoted:

> The governor, neatly attired in a black suit, hair immaculately coiffeured, emerged from University Hall relaxed and smiling to face several hundred long-haired students who had remained outside of a fenced parking lot where his Continental was parked for four hours.
> One car in the lot had already been pelted with eggs and two eggs smashed into the side of the governor's automobile as he came into view. Reagan waved cheerily as the crowd screamed obscenities and climbed inside while police pushed an opening in the throng. . . .
> Seeing the (governor's) vehicle stopped, the crowd suddenly surged into the street and went racing after it.
> The screaming mob had almost caught up when the light changed and the car moved along another block, only to get caught in some traffic.
> Sensing the possibilities, the mob poured down the middle of the street, raced through the light, which had turned red again, and were within a few feet of the car when an opening developed in the traffic and the vehicle spurted across Shattuck Avenue and out of reach. . . .

An exciting and detailed play-by-play, worthy of a Mel Allen or Dizzy Dean. If the same care had been lavished on the Regents' meeting, the story might have run to a prominent 60 or 70 inches, instead of the inside 13 it received.

Among the smaller papers, the Berkeley *Gazette* bannered "Eggs Thrown at Reagan Limousine Here." But the *Gazette* also ran two front-page stories totalling 54 inches on the meeting. The Vallejo *Times-Herald* led with the violence on page one, noting in an insert that a "related story" appeared on page two. The San Mateo *Times,* in the poorest showing of all, ran two front-page pictures of activists above the fold. A 10-inch story on page two sufficed for both demonstration and meeting coverage, the violence leading the story. The five paragraphs on the Regents were so superficial as to be meaningless. On January 18 the Palo Alto *Times* ran nothing at all on either the demonstration or the meeting.

This search for confrontation was not an isolated occurrence. On January 7 both the *Chronicle* and the Berkeley *Gazette* reported the peaceful opening of the College of San Mateo by focusing on arrests, warrants issued, and police checkpoints at the school. Not until the fifth paragraph of the *Gazette*'s story was the reader told: "Meanwhile, classes resumed without incident as 8,000 students at the racially troubled junior college returned from a two-week holiday recess . . ." There was no explanation in any paper of how the peaceful CSM opening was achieved.

Explaining and Clarifying

The problem of making sense of a continuing story, and the temptation to emphasize violence, could both have been mitigated had editors done a better job with interpretive and background stories on campus troubles. During the height of the confusion the *Chronicle* ran an editorial entitled "President and Press," which stated:

> The demands of the electronic and the printed media and their pressures are different. Television and radio have supplanted the press as the instantaneous transmitters to all corners of the world of words and deeds of statesmen. It is now the newspaper's role to explain and clarify.

Without exception, newspaper editors and executives interviewed by the authors agreed that this was indeed the role of the printed media, although some expressed mock amazement that the editorial appeared in the *Chronicle.* Many agreed that this was the role wherein newspapers had been most remiss. Said one *Chronicle* news executive, "This is the area where the *Chronicle* is most vulnerable and deserves to be criticized—for its lack of interpretive and depth coverage of the San

Francisco State crisis." But he pointed out that even the New York *Times* was guilty of the charge in its first five days of reporting the Columbia University takeover. "During the first five days the *Times* was reporting discrete events, and we were aware that they were missing the larger story—what was really going on."

Editor Mike Culbert, whose Berkeley *Gazette* has been grappling unsuccessfully with student coverage since the Free Speech Movement, agreed with the *Chronicle* editorial and added,

> There is a great frustration in realizing this need for interpretive reporting and not being able to do a thing about it. We did try to run a few pieces getting at the issues of the TWLF strike (at Berkeley) but I didn't have the resources to put on it. I would like to have had many more interpretive pieces.

Manpower problems hindering such reporting were equally severe at the San Mateo *Times* and the Vallejo *Times-Herald*.

The Oakland *Tribune*'s city editor, Roy Grimm, felt that newspapers "are making some progress in the direction of interpretation, although we have not shaken off the rush to get to the next edition." Grimm discussed a backstopping method also mentioned by *Examiner* city editor Gale Cook. Said Grimm, "If I feel we didn't do an adequate job with a story the first day, we'll follow up the next day with a story or fill in on Sunday." Cook also used Sunday as the place "to catch everyone up on what happened during the week at a more leisurely pace." In this connection, the *Chronicle*'s Champion believed that, "Every week to 10 days we should have done an analytical piece on the shifting state of events, so that the readers could get a clear assessment of it."

Harvey Yorke, Director of Public Affairs at San Francisco State College, has suggested another mechanism for upgrading the level of understanding and getting administration spokesmen "out of the propaganda business." Said Yorke,

> There needs to be a time for us to talk to newsmen without talking off the record, yet not making a story of everything that is said. We have to be able to tell them what we're thinking and planning without it showing up the next day in the paper as "The college is planning to do such-and-such."

It is a sad fact that one of the more ambitious interpretations written during the period appeared in the *Chronicle* on March 3, 1969, and came from the New York Times News Service. The *Times* had investigated the loss of faculty members at Berkeley and their return to East Coast schools because of the strike. Although the accuracy of the article has been questioned, the fact that the New York *Times* had to dig this information out in the Bay Area papers' own backyard is an unfavorable commentary on the imaginativeness of assignment editors. *Chronicle* editor Scott Newhall defended his paper by saying that "it is often easier for the *Chronicle* to run a story on Columbia than on Berkeley, because we're in the middle of it here." On the other hand, one doesn't see interpretive stories about Columbia in the *Chronicle,* or in any other Bay Area paper.

Bay Area reporters have become quite skilled in writing certain types of background and interpretive stories. The interview-profile has often been done with success. Donovan Bess of the *Chronicle* presented some valuable insights into the character and motivation of President Hayakawa in a January 2 interview at his Mill Valley home. The *Examiner*'s Rush Greenlee sketched Robert Hoover, center of controversy in the College of San Mateo's Readiness Program, in a December 23, 1968, story. The *Peninsula Observer,* a now-defunct weekly in Palo Alto that covered Peninsula affairs, was even more frank in its treatment of Hoover in a number of stories in December 1968, and January 1969.

Another approach was to turn news columns over to crisis participants either for short statements on a specific subject, or for a general airing of opinion. The "silent majorities" at SFS and Berkeley were not as silent as Governor Reagan and other critics of the student population would have the public believe. On December 8 the *Examiner* asked, "Why San Francisco State?" This question was presented to key actors in the crisis: State College Trustee Louis Heilbron; student body president Russell Bass; Glenn Smith, vice president of administrative and business affairs at SFS; Journalism Professor Jerrold Werthimer and others. Unfortunately, a maximum of only five or six paragraphs was allotted to any one source, making meaningful analysis impossible. Instead, each might have been given free rein, and the stories spread out into a daily series.

A third method was to turn the reporter into a selective "television camera" to describe what the campus looked like to him; how the air was charged, and what the expressions and feelings of the participants seemed to be, both on "normal" days and crisis days. Debates between two generations were popular playlets to write. Other material included banter between demonstrators and police, graffiti, crowd descriptions and accounts of innocent bystanders caught up in the action.

Although there was certainly a need for this type of reportage, it could not replace detailed probing into student demands, the history of the institution, past administration-student battles and conflicts in current negotiations. An *Examiner* article of January 7, headlined "An Almanac of Facts on SF State Crisis," was typical of the approach to these problems. Purporting, in bold type, to offer the "background" on the strike, the 29-inch piece presented the number of injuries, suspensions, arson attempts, bombings, police costs, class days lost and various monetary details. If this is background reporting, then one need only discuss the Vietnam war in terms of military hardware costs and the number killed and wounded.

Making Sense of "Demands"

Sets of demands were printed so often in Bay Area papers that the word "demand" may have become a cue for readers to flip to the comics. Yet how often were demands annotated in depth to enable the reader to make sense of them? Take, for example, the ten BSU (Black Students' Union) demands at San Francisco State, printed below:

That all Black studies courses being taught through various other departments be immediately part of the Black Studies Department and that all the instructors in this department receive full time pay.

That Dr. Nathan Hare, chairman of the Black Studies Department, receive a full professorship and a comparable salary according to his qualifications.

That there be a Department of Black Studies which will grant a bachelor's degree in Black Studies; that the Black Studies Department, chairman, faculty and staff have the sole power to hire faculty and control and determine the destiny of the department.

That all unused slots for Black students from fall, 1968 under the special admissions program be filled in spring, 1969.

That all Black students wishing to, be admitted in fall, 1969.

That 20 full time teaching positions be allocated to the Department of Black Studies.

That Dr. Helen Bedesem be replaced from the position of Financial Aid Officer and that a Black person be hired to direct it; that Third World people have the power to determine how it will be administered.

That no disciplinary action will be administered in any way to any students, workers, teachers, or administrators during and after the strike as a consequence of their participation in the strike.

That the California State College Trustees not be allowed to dissolve any Black programs on or off San Francisco State College campus.

That George Murray maintain his teaching position on campus for the 1968–69 academic year.

These demands suggested the following questions for major newspaper treatment. (1) In what ways would the Black Studies Department differ in organization from other academic departments? (2) How long have negotiations for a Black Studies Department been going on? What progress has been made? Which parties have been impeding progress, and why? (3) What would it cost to fund the Black Studies program, and where will the money come from? What was the cost of establishing other new departments at San Francisco State? How long did it take? From where did the money come? (4) What has led to the demand for replacement of Dr. Helen Bedesem as Financial Aid Officer? Answers to these questions were not available in Bay Area newspapers.

Some other matters that did not receive fully satisfactory explanations during the period under study included the order by Chancellor Glenn Dumke to suspend George Mason Murray; the role of the Coordinating Council for Higher Education; and the growth of the BSU on the campus. One was forced to the pages of *Ramparts,* the *Peninsula Observer,* and *Crisis* (a retrospective book published by SFS journalism students) for extended discussion of these issues.

Despite the massive space devoted to the strikes, Bay Area readers are probably no better prepared to understand the next student demonstration than they were the last. Too many of the stories were given over to trivial confrontations, arrests and pseudo-event rallies. Too few of them probed the "non-negotiable" positions on both sides. The Bay Area papers made laudable efforts to capture the emotion and drama of the strike—an almost impossible task. But they shirked some of the more feasible interpretive responsibilities.

Editors' Second Thoughts on Coverage

Discussions with many of the editors revealed some of the traps into which newspapers fell, and suggested means for improving coverage. The types of reporters sent to the demonstration, for example, and the order of their dispatch, had an important effect, especially on the early information gathering. Paul Conroy of the San Jose *News* said he first sent a police reporter; after the violence subsided, he assigned an education writer to determine why it happened. Roy Grimm of the Oakland *Tribune* acknowledged that "perhaps we take too much of the police beat approach to these things, and get too involved in the running battle."

A *Chronicle* editor was convinced that "the basic pattern of covering a strike at SFS is what causes trouble." He continued,

> First you react to the story with a stringer who is on the scene, on whom you have relied in the past. Then a little violence starts and you send over some reporters who are experienced at reporting headknocking. Then you start to run the handouts from the President's office. Only late in the game do you recognize what kind of story it is and begin to report it properly.

One need not minimize or condone the violence involved in campus demonstrations, to suggest that it would be better if education writers and campus specialists such as the *Examiner's* Phil Garlington (now covering Sacramento), Lynn Ludlow, and Lance Gilmore, the *News's* Rick Egner and the *Chronicle's* Ron Moskowitz, be given greater responsibility. They could take some of the burden from police reporters, stringers (usually students on the paper's payroll who supply information to the staff reporter), and plants (part-timers assigned by the paper to carry out a specific job, e.g., posing as student demonstrators. This system was used by the Berkeley *Gazette*).

The five large papers and the Berkeley *Gazette* seemed to be minimally prepared in advance with either full-timers or stringers on the campuses in their area. The *Examiner,* for example, had full-time men at San Francisco State and Berkeley, a part-timer at Stanford, plus great faith in Stanford's News Bureau chief Bob Beyers (a regard shared by many other editors). The *Mercury-News* had two reporters at San Jose State, and the *Gazette* had one and a half full-time people, four stringers, and three plants at Berkeley, in what is a massive operation for a small paper. The Palo Alto *Times* had no stringer at Stanford, however, and the *Chronicle* and *Examiner* could each spare only a reporter for one day to gather background on the Stanford sit-in. Naturally, one could hope for more education news from the campuses before a confrontation starts, but such forecasting of trouble is extremely risky, readership is low and editors have difficulty finding the space.

The Press and Student Activists

Despite some advance planning, many papers were unable to establish a rapport with student militants. "Students were oriented to the TV press conference, [rather than to the newspaper interview]" said the *Examiner's* Gale Cook. "It was hard to get a statement from them, and when you did, you still didn't know if it was representative of campus sentiment." Kenneth Conn, executive editor of the *Mercury-News,* agreed. "It was hard to talk to student dissidents. As members of the Establishment we couldn't do it. They didn't trust us." Roy Grimm speculated that his reporters were hampered by the conservative reputation of the *Tribune's* owner, former Senator William Knowland. Such experiences suggest a marked reversal from the Berkeley FSM (Free Speech Movement) days in 1964, when, as a former University administrator reminisced, "In those days, the students were nothing if not articulate. If they won't talk to the press now, that is a distinct change."

Because of the access problem, there was a clear superiority in coverage of the participation of the American Federation of Teachers over the student participation. This was particularly true in the *Chronicle,* where one can only wish that former labor writer Dick Meister's excellent AFT coverage had been repeated for the students. Journalism professor and AFT member Jerrold Werthimer ground out AFT press releases during the strike, and had no complaints over press coverage. There was some evidence that radical communication experts among the students began to make a concerted effort at helping the press obtain strike information. This was the case at the Applied Electronics Laboratory sit-in at Stanford in April 1969. Students were assigned to shepherd reporters around the site, answer questions, suggest leads and features and do everything else a good public relations man must do. Reporters were, on the average, receptive and cooperative and strike coverage was somewhat improved.

It is imperative that relations between student activists and establishment papers be improved. The *Chronicle's* Dale Champion pointed out chillingly that papers "have portrayed student dissidents as the enemy." He believed that many college administrators are desirous of instituting changes, but any innovations are seen as a capitulation to demonstrators, whom the public views as the enemy. This is a dangerous situation.

Because they often were unable to obtain information from militants or mediators, reporters frequently became pipelines for the establishment-administration viewpoint, which angered students. The San Jose *News's* Dick Egner often opened the news pages of his paper to San Jose State President Robert D. Clark for comment on the AFT strike. In a 22-inch story on January 2, headlined "SJS Faculty Strike Plan 'Baseless,' " Clark not only described the demands of San Jose State's AFT chapter, but also told why each demand was spurious or indicated how it was already being remedied. Not one AFT spokesman was quoted. The Vallejo *Times-Herald* failed to pursue any of the leads provided by Solano College President N. Dallas Evans in municipal court testimony about a sit-in disturbance at the college. Defense counsel for the 19 Negro student defendants, Robert K. Winters, allegedly caught Evans in distortions and mis-statements of fact, yet the paper failed to investigate the sit-in, beyond using the official channels.

Wire Services and TV

Among Bay Area editors and executives there was unanimous agreement on the extremely poor quality of wire service coverage of local disorders. This was particularly evident in AP and UPI stories on student demonstrations. Repeatedly wire stories overplayed the head-knocking, the sensational and the bizarre. They did not provide the types of background-interpretive pieces that staffs of the larger papers turned out. The *News's* Paul Conroy—along with Vallejo publisher Luther Gibson, has complained for 20 years about the deteriorating quality of San Francisco wire coverage. The wire services' treatment of the demonstrations was unimaginative and superficial. The Berkeley *Gazette's* Mike Culbert was most vocal in his criticism. "AP and UPI could not even be relied on to report the headknocking correctly," said Culbert. "The wire services didn't know what was going on in the first stages of the TWLF [Third World Liberation Front] strike [at Berkeley]. The early leads in the first days of the strike were atrocious. At one point AP was taking down my *speculation* on what was happening and moving it as the early lead." It should be remembered that a wire service staff is about one-tenth the size of the *Examiner* or *Chronicle* news staff.

Poor wire coverage hurt such papers as the Santa Rosa *Press-Democrat,* San Mateo *Times,* Vallejo *Times-Herald,* Palo Alto *Times* and Berkeley *Gazette* much more than it did the big five dailies. The latter were at least able to cover major demonstrations on a regular basis. When a smaller paper could free one of its own men for duty, such as for the opening of SFS after the Christmas cooling off period, the results were not happy. Said San Mateo *Times* publisher J. Hart Clinton, "We sent a reporter and a photographer to SFS but they might as well have stayed at home. Covering SFS and similar disturbances requires more sophisticated people than we have working in the news room." Stories turned in on the January 7 reopening of SFS by the *Press-Democrat's* Peter Golis and the Palo Alto *Times's* Ron Goben and Ken Rowe contained much of the same material moved by the wire services that day. Golis described in rather pedestrian terms the "scene" at Nineteenth and Holloway (SFS), and threw in some press conference quotes from SFS President Hayakawa and AFT President Gary Hawkins for good measure. Goben and Rowe did virtually the same thing. The *Times's* story ran 18 inches, the *Press-Democrat's* only 16. Clearly both the papers and the readers were shortchanged.

Pressure on Editors

In the future, manpower allocation by both large and small dailies will represent important policy decisions. The two San Francisco papers frequently had up to 10 men assigned to the student story. "It was a real drain on our resources," said the *Examiner's* Gale Cook. Roy Grimm of the *Tribune* called it "damn expensive coverage"; and the *Mercury's* Kenneth Conn said such coverage "pulled other reporters off their beats, burned up many columns of our news hole, and lost

us a lot of time just keeping people on alert." Part of this may be due
to what Cook called "the escalation effect." He said, "We all got caught
up in one of those things where it's a question of who is going to be
the first one to let go of the story. But each paper was afraid of getting
beaten if they did let go. This had an escalation effect on the coverage."
Despite this, two editors—German and Culbert—plan to send in more
manpower earlier for the next demonstration.

Another, more visible, pressure on editors came from television.
Grimm, Cook, and Vallejo managing editor Wyman Riley knew that
the local television stations would feature the headknocking on their
evening news reports. They felt impelled to follow television's lead
in their own news presentations. "If you know what TV is going to
show that evening," said Grimm, "you feel you have to show it too."

The great difficulty in portraying campus events accurately and
fairly has been pointed out by two members of the Berkeley faculty—
Joseph Lyford and Spencer Klaw. Klaw, a former associate editor of
Fortune magazine, believed it would have taken "instant historical interpretation to put all the events in place, which is too much to ask
of the medium." Lyford and Klaw invited 60 of their students to submit papers on what the TWLF strike at Berkeley meant to them, and
Lyford found some interesting opinions that defended the press. "Many
student papers criticized the media for reporting so much violence at
the expense of other kinds of coverage," Lyford said. "But we noted
that about 90 percent of the comments made by students in their
papers were concerned with violence and the reaction to it, so perhaps
the violence was more important than some people think."

Another student pointed out that the *Daily Californian*—which was
in sympathy with the strike, like most student newspapers—was just
as guilty as its bigger cousins in failing to report the background issues.
In the months before the actual strike began, the University administration and various minority organizations were negotiating at length on
setting up a Black studies program in a Third World College. The
Daily Californian reported none of this, concentrating instead on the
issue of credit for Eldridge Cleaver's proposed course 139X. The *Daily
Californian*, like the rest of the media, paid sole attention to what was
happening at the moment. Because of the silence concerning TWLF-
Administration negotiations, when the strike started many U.C. students were uninformed as to why there was a strike, on what issues the
students and the administration differed, and on what had already
occurred. If Berkeley students were confused, is it any wonder that Bay
Area newspaper readers were confused?

It is encouraging that most editors admit their failings in presenting interpretive pieces, overplaying the violence, and identifying too closely with the Establishment. Most are also aware that the age difference between editors and demonstrators makes it difficult, as Scott Newhall says, "for editors to know what in hell the kids are thinking." Another *Chronicle* editor described "a very live argument currently raging at the *Chronicle*" over the best way to cover demonstrations: is it to be the interpretive, lengthy, more personal article in the Norman Mailer-John Hersey-Truman Capote style of reporting; or is it to be the more old-fashioned, straight news reporting, with the elusive standard of objectivity? The *Chronicle* leans to the former. The other papers do not seem to have reached this stage yet. But the problems created in covering student demonstrations have begun to obscure the distinction between "article" and "news story." The *Chronicle*'s German has expressed willingness to break the stereotypes of traditional news coverage. Moreover, pouring the 1968–1969 student revolt into the old news molds may have irreparably cracked the molds. The new methods that editors and reporters adopt will affect media coverage of all events.

Case Study: Regional Organization and the Environmental Crisis

In the past few years, the proliferation of Bay Area citizens' groups that fight the redwood loggers, Bay fillers, air polluters, and even the Army Corps of Engineers, has testified to the environmental awareness of Californians. Elected officials in the nine-county Bay Area have demonstrated a willingness—unmatched in many other urban areas— to examine regional problems of transportation, open space, air quality, water pollution, sewage and related ecological matters. Witness the many "alphabet" commissions in the Bay Area, including: The San Francisco Bay Conservation and Development Commission (BCDC), the Bay Area Air Pollution Control District (BAAPCD), San Francisco Bay-Delta Water Quality Control Study (Bay-Delta), The Bay Area Transportation Study Committee (BATS), the Association of Bay Area Governments (ABAG) and others.

The Story of the '70's

A gathering of journalists in late June, 1969, arranged by Stanford's Professional Journalism Fellows program, heard former ABC commentator and chief correspondent of the Public Broadcast Laboratory Edward P. Morgan offer this perspective on inadequate environmental coverage by the daily press. "In the 1950's," he said, "the big story was reporting the cold war. Reporters completely missed the major stories of the 1960's: the Negro revolution and campus unrest. I wonder what the major story of the 1970's will be that the press has failed to report?" Morgan answered his own question—he believed it would be environmental deterioration.

Among the many academicians who agree with Morgan is Joseph Lyford, Professor of Journalism at Berkeley. Lyford believes that the reporting of "environmental aggression" stories is the chief current duty of a newspaper. "If such stories are not covered because they are invisible, or because there is no news peg, then we may face irreversible ecological erosion in the years ahead."

The genuine conservationist spirit in the Bay Area, manifested in a prevailing sense of urgency about ecological matters that is in the vanguard of American sentiment, encourages the expectation that Bay Area newspapers would be enterprising in their environmental coverage. Although the overall picture has yet to be determined, there are many definitely bright spots. The Oakland *Tribune*'s Fred Garretson

128

and the San Jose *Mercury*'s Tom Harris (now writing in place of Bailey and Cannon) have earned recognized and respected by-lines in environmental reporting.[1] Among the better environmental writers is Harold Gilliam, who writes twice each month for the *Chronicle*'s Sunday magazine; Paul Peterzell of the San Rafael *Independent-Journal;* Scott Thurber of the *Chronicle;* and Al Cline of the *Examiner,* all of whom do what they can in a limited amount of time.

But most papers and almost all broadcast stations do not have the manpower or the will to staff regularly the many meetings of regulatory agencies that bear responsibility for quality of the environment. Many such meetings are covered by only one or two papers, if at all. The wire services contribute little.

Bay Area Regional Organization

Many ecological problems tend to be peculiar to one area, making it difficult to deliver an overall evaluation of environmental coverage in Bay Area newspapers. Instead, we have chosen coverage of a regional issue of uniform importance to all nine counties: the report of the Joint Committee on Bay Area Regional Organization (popularly known as BARO), chaired by Assemblyman John T. Knox. The committee was charged by the California State Legislature with "studying the possibilities of establishing a regional organization in the San Francisco Bay Area to insure the region's effective and orderly planning, growth, and development in conjunction with the conservation of its physical and environmental resources." The joint committee went out of existence at the end of the 1970 session of the California Legislature, but Bay Area regional organization is still a lively issue.[2]

In a massive investigation, the joint committee considered the following multi-county, multi-jurisdictional concerns to evaluate the desirability and feasibility of incorporating them into some form of regional governmental organization:

> Regional planning;
> Air and water pollution;
> Solid waste disposal;
> Regional parks and open space;
> Transportation, including airports, bridges, rapid transit and ports;
> The socio-economic impact and desirability of regional government;
> The necessary powers required for a regional government to function effectively;

---

[1] Gilbert Bailey, who did a good job on the environmental beat for the *Mercury,* now works for the Long Beach *Independent Press-Telegram.*

[2] We monitored the newspapers for the BARO story for the period from December 23, 1968 to March 4, 1969. Basic data are drawn primarily from this period.

Membership composition and selective methods for said regional government;

Methods for including existing regional and sub-regional multi-county districts and agencies, where appropriate, into said new regional government;

The determination of an appropriate definition for "the San Francisco Bay Area" with respect to regional organization; and

All other functional matters relevant to regional organization.

Clearly the legislative recommendations resulting from this study should have held a high interest for all papers in the Bay Area. At a December 17, 1968 press conference, Assemblyman Knox first unveiled his plan for a Bay Area regional government (also rather ambiguously referred to by the same acronym as the Joint Committee, BARO). The Joint Committee report was complex and required thoughtful interpretation and careful explanation. In response, all of the 10 papers on which our study focused carried prominent, and frequently lengthy, articles on the proposal.

How effective was the newspapers' treatment of the story? In part this is an unfair question, because the first agent controlling the flow of information was the committee's public information officer, C. Dennis Orphan, a former newsman in Baltimore and Chicago. Orphan wrestled with the problem of presenting the committee findings to the press so that the information would be intelligible to reporters, and subsequently to the readers. "Most papers do not have the staff to interpret a 150-page report and present it to the public," said Orphan. "If I do a digest of the report, I'll be guilty of imposing my judgment of what is important on the papers." Orphan tentatively thought of preparing a different digest for each of the nine counties, emphasizing points of local interest, but in the end, under deadline pressure, he issued a single 15-page report.

Orphan first outlined the four general functions of the proposed regional government: (1) taking over the functions of BCDC; (2) beginning work on a billion-dollar regional sewage facility; (3) designating major transportation corridors for the region; and (4) acquiring and operating regional parks and open space. Next he presented a section on organizational detail, including officers, salaries and standing committees.

He then listed the powers and duties of the proposed regional government, beginning with a description of the general regional plan to be prepared. The nucleus of the plan would consist of five mandatory elements—relating to transportation, environmental quality, regional parks and open space, San Francisco Bay and public service facilities. Eight additional factors of less importance which the plan should contain were also outlined. Next came specific land use powers with respect to the Bay, and a statement concerning control over policy and management of other existing agencies to be exercised by the regional government. The report closed with a brief statement of possible revenue sources to finance the regional government, including an income surtax, sales and use taxes, environmental quality fees, and general obligation and revenue bonds. Although this outline is sketchy, it gives some idea of the scope and emphasis of Orphan's report, which none of the papers printed in full.

Newspaper Attitudes and the Gatekeeper's Role

Despite the fact that reporters were virtually handed the basis for their stories in Orphan's short report, each paper's policy on the regional government question, and on environmental problems in general, played an important gatekeeper role.[3] Stories on December 17 and 18, 1968 appeared as banner leads, above the paper's name in the Berkeley *Gazette*, with red headlines in the Oakland *Tribune*, as a page one second lead in the San Jose *Mercury*, on page 14 in the San Francisco *Examiner*, and as far back as page 36 in the San Jose *News*.

The *Mercury*'s Gil Bailey called the regional organization a "controversial" proposal with "broad power over local governments." The San Francisco *Chronicle*'s Mike Harris saw it as "a series of gentle steps . . . toward the formation of limited regional government. . . ." Fred Wyatt of the Berkeley *Gazette* called it "a sweeping proposal." The Oakland *Tribune* devoted 86 inches to the proposal in two days; the Vallejo *Times-Herald* 51 inches on December 18; the *Chronicle* 33 inches; the *Examiner* 30; the San Mateo *Times* 18 inches; and the Santa Rosa *Press-Democrat* a paltry 11 inches. Clearly it made a great difference which reporter in which paper one read, when seeking information even of the relatively simplified press-conference variety. It also indicated that Orphan was probably correct in his judgment that at least the suburban papers could not adequately deal with a 150-page report.

The Oakland *Tribune* and Fred Garretson presented by far the most complete and accurate stories. The *Tribune* was the best Bay Area paper for environmental coverage, largely because of Garretson's work. The day of the conference, the *Tribune* ran a 34-inch story on page one outlining the Knox recommendations in rather value-free terms. Garretson acted essentially as a conduit: he included verbatim the five mandatory elements of the report; the general functions; and

---

[3] With respect to newspapers, the gatekeeper is one who decides which items shall be admitted to a place in the columns, and which items shall be excluded.

some of the material on powers and responsibility, financing, and organization. The next day—and this was the crucial element—Garretson brought his own special expertise to bear in an analytical piece of 52 inches. With intelligence and perception he discussed the need for a regional framework; he outlined the agencies that most likely would be subsumed under BARO; and he posed the question of power levels in Washington, Sacramento, the regional level and the local level. No other paper matched this one-two punch of careful reporting and close analysis.

In its own disturbing way the *Mercury-News* came the closest to the *Tribune*. On December 17 Gil Bailey wrote for the *News* a 22-inch factual report of the BARO proposal, containing most of the essential information. In the *Mercury* the next morning Bailey wrote an analytical piece slightly hostile to BARO, but full of his knowledgeable observations. He discussed potential points of controversy raised by the proposal and questioned the costs involved. It was the necessary companion piece to the *News* article. Unfortunately, they appeared in two different newspapers that do not have full circulation overlap. What the 50,000 or so *Mercury* readers who did not subscribe to the *News* made of Bailey's analytical piece (and therefore of the BARO proposal) is hard to say. Readers taking only one or the other of the two papers were shortchanged. This happens often with the *Mercury-News* combination.

With one exception, the other Bay Area papers either presented the story without analytical comment, or mixed the two in one piece. Both approaches were inferior to that taken by the *Tribune*. The services of an expert in this area are essential if a paper hopes to comment intelligently about future BAROs. Former *Gazette* reporter Fred Wyatt and the Palo Alto *Times's* Jay Thorwaldson were clearly in too deep in an admittedly complex subject. The *Chronicle's* Michael Harris presented more of his own views on regional government than those of Assemblyman Knox. The *Examiner's* H. W. Kusserow, wrote a good, factual piece on December 17, but there was no follow-up story.

At least, however, the above-mentioned papers recognized the importance of the story, and had representatives at the press conference. In contrast, the San Mateo *Times,* Santa Rosa *Press-Democrat,* and Vallejo *Times-Herald* used wire stories that were dull and perfunctory. For the *Times,* in an area already bursting with fill projects and related controversy, this was inexcusable. The *Times-Herald's* use of AP was disturbing for a different reason. Publisher Luther Gibson attacked the BARO proposal with a vengeance. Most other Bay Area papers ran one or two editorials on the subject from December 1968 to March 1969 (with the exception of the San Mateo *Times*, which ran none).

But the Gibson papers carried lengthy denunciations of BARO on December 21, December 27, December 31, January 27, February 20, March 4 and March 18. As expected, Gibson opposed the concept because of his stated fear that less populous areas, such as Sonoma, Solano and Napa counties, would be dominated by the larger urban areas and would be dragged into problems of neither their concern nor making. The editorials argued this position, and challenged the one man-one vote, majority rule approach taken by Knox. Gibson also asked for local option on joining the regional government. Journalistically this was a perfectly reasonable position, and because managing editor Wyman Riley admitted that reader interest in the issue (judging by letters to the editor) was very low, the Gibson papers were probably smart to crusade in order to build interest in the subject. But Riley knew what to expect from the Knox committee, and he owed Vallejo readers more than a 15-inch AP story, countered by 36 inches from local Assemblyman John F. Dunlap, a member of the Knox committee, who registered his criticisms (juxtaposed with the AP article). The arguments presented by Dunlap and the newspaper editorials were indistinguishable.

Presentation of the Amended BARO Proposal

In Sacramento on March 3, Assemblyman Knox formally presented newsmen an amended legislative proposal for regional government. Only the articles by the *Tribune*'s Ed Salzman and the *Chronicle*'s Sacramento bureau made the connection between the December proposal and the March revision. The rest of the papers (with the exception of the Vallejo *Times-Herald*) either used wire service copy or wire copy disguised as Sacramento bureau stories. The regional government story was sufficiently complicated without newspapers adding to the confusion by presenting the March proposal as something discrete from the December proposal. Only the *Tribune* and *Chronicle* handled the story properly: they described the revisions; summarized the basic provisions and assessed the political chances of the bill. Wire stories concentrated on organization of the government—all old material— and presented the five mandatory elements of the regional plan as if they were new.

The Vallejo *Times-Herald* used the occasion as a news peg on which to present more of Assemblyman Dunlap's negative views. Following is the *Times-Herald*'s coverage of the Knox press conference—the page two story ran four-and-a-half inches:

Dunlap Opposes Knox Proposal

Assemblyman John Dunlap, D-Napa, yesterday told his opposition to a bill by Assemblyman John Knox, D-Richmond, calling for formation of a limited super-government in the Bay Area, Dunlap said:

"Despite the fact that this bill changes the so-called staff report recommendation so that the area of the proposed regional agency would exclude Dixon, Rio Vista and Vacaville, I still am opposed to it.

"Its provisions for a referendum are based on a regional referendum rather than one which will allow local communities, including counties or cities, to decide individually for themselves whether they want in or out.

"Although I have always recognized that we have regional problems, I don't think we can solve them by a mandatory regional government. I think the people have to want something before it's going to work."

It would be virtually impossible for a reader to piece together the facts of Knox's March proposal from such an article as this.

Beyond the December and March press conferences, coverage of regional government followed the same patterns already established. At the top, the Oakland *Tribune* ran an excellent piece in its Sunday, December 3, 1968, "Metropolitan News Section" describing all the existing agencies with overlapping regional authority. The article was accompanied by a diagram of regional authority over Oakland which made the picture quite comprehensible. On December 25 Garretson presented a report by Stanley Scott and John Bollens, published by the University of California's Institute of Governmental Studies at Berkeley. The report tended to support main elements of the Knox proposal. Garretson followed this on December 29 with a discussion of regional government in the Minneapolis-St. Paul area, and showed how the Twin Cities' experience might be applicable to Bay Area problems. The *Tribune* periodically reviewed the status of the Knox proposal, covered debates on regional government throughout the Bay Area, and reported the changes in the Knox proposal a week before the second press conference.

The *Mercury-News*'s Gil Bailey also discussed the Twin Cities Metropolitan Council in a January 7 piece. A lengthy article on December 22, headed "Just What Is Regional Government?" provided a valuable analysis of overlapping regional authorities, much like Fred Garretson's. Urban affairs writer Jack Fraser (who also has since left San Jose) contributed a couple of sharp political analyses of the Knox proposal, plus information on the philosophy of the Bay Area Council's Citizens for Active Discussion of Regional Organization (CADRO). The subsequent departure of Bailey and Fraser is reflected in the poor March coverage offered by the *Mercury-News*. Executive editor Kenneth Conn was hard pressed to replace these two until he hired Tom Harris.

From December through March neither the *Examiner* nor the *Chronicle* provided anything comparable to the work of Garretson and Bailey. The *Examiner* even used AP for its March 3 story on Knox. Of the smaller papers only the *Times-Herald,* which was printing every anti-Knox comment it could find, gave any attention to the matter. On December 19, Don Engdahl of the Santa Rosa *Press-Democrat* wrote an excellent 40-inch piece analyzing the Knox proposal from the perspective of the northern counties, but the *Press-Democrat*'s article of March 3 may as well have been written the previous December. Coverage in the San Mateo *Times,* Palto Alto *Times* and Berkeley *Gazette* was also weak.

In dealing with the issue of regional government, the newspapers treated the matter in a mixed and uneven way, a circumstance not entirely of their own creation. Some of the problems surrounding the BARO report are suggested by this statement made by a knowledgeable reporter who attempted to cover the BARO story:

> The BARO report, commissioned when the 1969 legislative fight appeared likely to concern regional government rather than the future of the Bay Conservation and Development Commission (BCDC), was badly goofed up and seriously delayed, although many of the fine young men and women who were dragooned to work on sections of it probably didn't know this. The report was actually supposed to have been prepared months before, and was to have been much more of a blueprint for action than it actually turned out.

By March 3, when an amended proposal was issued, many viewed it as being largely window dressing and were convinced that the battle had shifted to saving BCDC.

> Knox was the commander in the latter fight and deserves the credit he got for "saving the Bay." But what should have been reported on BARO . . . was that the deadline for the report had not been met, that the nature of the report (some of it still in "notes") was far different from what had been promised, that the committee work was in a mess, and that the Legislature had given up on the proposal for the time being, both because of the lobbyist counter-attack on BCDC and their dissatisfaction with the progress of BARO. Knox, who was just beginning to take the steps in behalf of BCDC that ultimately proved so decisive, received a lot of favorable free publicity for BARO . . . and then put the report on ice, where it was destined to go anyway.

The Chronicle, the Tribune and the Environmental Beat

While, in retrospect, the entire BARO idea gave way to the fight to save the Bay Conservation and Development Commission, the type of treatment it received is important if one is to understand the generally uneven coverage given environmental matters by the Bay Area press.

Are all alphabet reports from government and university commissions handled in such a fashion? Will only a crisis such as the Santa Barbara oil slick prompt detailed coverage? Can the press be expected to provide some sort of early warning system on environmental matters? These are just some of the questions that could be answered by detailed study of media performance in reporting air and water pollution, over-population, urban crowding, mass transit and solid waste disposal. A small step in this direction has been provided by Penny Hermes, a Berkeley graduate student with a background in biology and journalism. From December 1968, through March 1969, Miss Hermes compared the coverage of air and water pollution stories in the *Chronicle* and *Tribune*. Her conclusions tended to support those presented above.

"During this period," she said, "the *Tribune* ran three times as many stories as the *Chronicle* on those subjects, with 920 more column inches. The *Tribune* has three writers (including Garretson) on the environmental beat, while the *Chronicle* has only Scott Thurber." Miss Hermes believes that the *Tribune* considered such stories to be of high priority, while the *Chronicle* played them down because they were not "sexy" or interesting enough. *Tribune* city editor Roy Grimm is convinced that one of the reasons his paper is considered dull or drab by some critics is its emphasis on complex environmental stories. "The problem with material like that is making it readable," said Grimm. But the *Tribune* has been willing to pay the price, whereas the *Chronicle* has not.

When the *Chronicle* did take notice of such questions, its coverage was discontinuous, and lacked both backgrounding and follow-up. The *Chronicle* was especially negligent in its coverage of Bay pollution by San Francisco's sewage system. The *Tribune* began covering this story in December; the *Chronicle* did not pick it up until March 12.

Miss Hermes also contended that the *Chronicle* has avoided some controversial issues that would have required stepping on the toes of influential persons. She said that the paper has steadily failed to report the maneuverings of West Bay Community Associates, the group that is hoping to fill part of San Mateo County's shoreline for tract housing. Garretson, in contrast, has consistently named names in his stories. He told Miss Hermes that during one of his series, publisher William Knowland told him to be even more specific and to name even more names. The fact that the late Joseph R. Knowland, Sr., and his wife were among the founders of the Save the Bay Association and were active on the Save the Redwoods campaign and the California State Park Commission has influenced the *Tribune*'s coverage.

Echoing many editors, Miss Hermes criticized AP and UPI for unexciting coverage of environmental issues. "They do no digging on their own," she said. "They read the *Chronicle* in the morning and pick up what they have. Very little of what the *Tribune* does gets on to the wire, so almost nothing of interest gets outside the Bay Area."

One man can have much influence on the quality of wire coverage of the environment in the Bay Area. The *Tribune*'s Fred Garretson reported that while Doug Willis of AP was assigned to the local environmental beat in mid-1969, he did an excellent job. When Willis was transferred to Sacramento, however, coverage returned to its usual level.

Regional environmental stories are impossible for the wires to cover using present methods, anyway. Since so much wire coverage of all types of stories is a rewrite of the metro papers, a rewrite of a story of regional importance would require the wire man to gather local reports from papers all around the Bay in order to put the story in a perspective of regional interest. If this were done (which it is not) the story would be one or two days old—too old for other papers in the state or the West to carry.

Miss Hermes also criticized all Bay Area papers for not regularly covering the air and water pollution control agency meetings. "The *Chronicle* won't travel to Oakland for meetings, and the *Tribune* won't go into San Francisco."

The Santa Barbara Oil Leak Story

The oil well leak in the Santa Barbara Channel was surely one of the most significant environmental pollution stories of the decade, particularly for California. Nevertheless, none of the Bay Area papers covered the story with their own reporters, although all ran varying amounts of wire copy. The authors examined this coverage in six of the Bay papers, and the New York *Times,* for the two-week period February 17 to March 4, 1969. Tables 7 and 8 present (1) the total number of column inches each paper ran on the Santa Barbara oil slick story and, for comparison, on the Sirhan trial, which was another California-based event that received only wire coverage in Bay Area papers; (2) the number of days (out of a total of 14) a story appeared; and (3) the number of times a story appeared in the first four pages of the paper.

The two tables showed that, judging by the attention it received, the oil slick story ranked just behind the Sirhan trial in perceived news value. It was most significant that the continuity of coverage of the oil slick story was comparable to that of the Sirhan trial. Editors recognized the importance of the story, gave it space almost every day for

TABLE 7

OIL LEAK: SUMMARY OF TREATMENT IN SIX BAY AREA DAILIES AND
THE NEW YORK TIMES, FEBRUARY 17–MARCH 4, 1969

Paper	Total column inches	No. of days in paper	No. of days on first four pages
San Francisco *Chronicle*	265	13	10
San Jose *Mercury*	222	12	5
New York *Times*	191	7	5
Vallejo *Times-Herald*	147	12	4
Oakland *Tribune*	131	11	2
San Francisco *Examiner*	130	10	4
Berkeley *Gazette*	25	4	2

TABLE 8

SIRHAN TRIAL: SUMMARY OF TREATMENT IN SIX BAY AREA DAILIES AND
THE NEW YORK TIMES, FEBRUARY 17–MARCH 4, 1969

Paper	Total column inches	No. of days in paper	No. of days on first four pages
New York *Times*	435	11	3
San Jose *Mercury*	381	11	8
San Francisco *Chronicle*	272	12	2
Vallejo *Times-Herald*	241	12	11
Oakland *Tribune*	209	13	9
San Francisco *Examiner*	148	10	3
Berkeley *Gazette*	128	10	4

two weeks, and frequently featured it in the first four pages. During this period the Pueblo investigation, the Presidio "mutiny" trial, and the Mid-east crisis all received daily coverage of lesser magnitude than the Santa Barbara oil slick.

With the exception of the Berkeley *Gazette,* which virtually ignored the oil slick, Bay Area papers seemed receptive to covering stories of an ecological nature. The current problem is that editors are not taking the initiative in seeking out and exposing instances of what Joseph Lyford called "environmental aggression." When a federal task force indicated it would help California groups in preventing tampering with San Francisco Bay, the papers reacted with varying coverage. When a group of experts issued a report citing the dangers of continued Bay pollution, papers gave the story prominent space for a day and then moved on. This is normal, long-standing newspaper practice.

Covering the ecological and environmental story, however, demands a more dynamic newspaper ethic. The urgency of the environmental issue, and the danger of waiting for news pegs on which to hang environmental stories at a time when the problems are festering all around must lead to new approaches.

The AP's Bill Stall, inspired by William Bronson's book *How to Kill a Golden State* (Garden City, N.Y.: Doubleday, 1968), wrote a three-part series that ran in the San Jose *News* and Palo Alto *Times* on January 13, 14 and 15, 1969. An editor's note to the first piece explained Stall's purpose: "For nearly 200 years, man has exploited California's natural resources in an effort to build and live 'the good life.' Here is the first of three articles on how Californians now are trying to repair the scars of that exploitation." Stall briefly touched on the philosophical differences between Dr. Edgar Wayburn of the Sierra Club and Larry Kiml, natural resources director for the State Chamber of Commerce; zoning along Interstate 5; slum conditions and pollution at Lake Tahoe; comprehensive city planning by the Irvine Company in Southern California; and smog and motor vehicle pollution. This kind of series, but done in much greater depth, would help focus attention on local environmental and ecological problems. Stall had no news peg and no specific axe to grind, yet the series presented a readable and valuable overview of California's problems.

Priority Concerns of Weekly and Monthly Papers

Many of the area's weekly and monthly newspapers have made environmental problems one of their top priority concerns—and consequently are far outstripping the daily newspapers. The *Freedom News,* Richmond's monthly alternative to the daily *Independent,* has done much that is worth imitating. Contributor Clifford C. Humphrey writes regularly on the "Politics of Ecology," and in the April 1969 issue he covered the Sierra Club Wilderness Conference in detail. The May 1969 issue had a special supplement titled "Diagnosis of San Francisco Bay," which offered a detailed map showing Bay fill plans; a discussion of such Bay Area concerns as earthquakes, refuse, open space and the Bay-Delta Plan; and the names and addresses of all Bay Area groups concerned with environmental problems.

Freedom News editor Betty Segal has also challenged Standard Oil for its "wreaking" of Richmond (February 1969) and criticized a redevelopment project for downtown Richmond (October 1968). The paper is militantly protective of the East Bay environment, and it is performing a service for its community that the *Chronicle, Examiner, Mercury* and *News* are shirking in their respective cities.

Mrs. Segal admitted that the *Freedom News* borrowed many of its ideas for environmental coverage from the defunct *Peninsula Observer*, a Palo Alto weekly edited by David Ransom. Although the strict revolutionary left "line" of the *Observer* prejudiced much of its political coverage and affected the overall credibility of the newspaper, its air pollution coverage by Ned Groth was first rate. In a series of articles beginning on November 18, 1968, Groth took a hard look at the Bay Area Air Pollution Control District and what it was not doing. In the November 18 cover story, entitled "Breathing More Now and Enjoying It Less?" Groth assessed the regulatory spirit of the commission and its close links to the industries it was created to regulate. He also published a list of leading smog makers in the Bay Area.

On January 6, Groth turned to Los Altos Hills' pollution problem caused by the Kaiser-Permanente Cement Company, a subject also tackled by the Los Altos *Town Crier*. Uncontrolled emissions from Kaiser's clinker-coolers were settling as a fine powder all over the south Peninsula. Groth moved on to the Monterey area in the January 20 issue to examine pollution from the PG&E steam-generator electric power plant at Moss Landing. The dangers of fluoride pollution from industrial smoke stacks received his fire on January 27. Next to the "coming revolution," the *Observer* made control of environmental pollution its top priority concern, and Bay Area dailies (especially on the Peninsula) could have learned much from it.

The Burlingame *Advance-Star*, the twice-a-week sister paper of the daily Palo Alto *Times* and Redwood City *Tribune*, provided further evidence that the nondailies can do an excellent job in this area. The Sunday, March 2, 1969 issue provided a better advance story on the Knox proposal in Sacramento than most papers ran *following* the news conference. A banner story on February 9 explained the controversy between the Bay Conservation and Development Commission and San Mateo Senator Richard J. Dolwig. The bylined story by George Newman also provided a map of the Bay (reprinted from *California Tomorrow*) depicting lands already diked or filled and potentially fillable Bay lands. The following week the *Advance-Star* ran the official Bay Plan map submitted to the state legislature by the BCDC, picturing waterfront land uses that would be allowed under the plan.

If Bay Area dailies had the enthusiasm and sense of urgency pervading these weeklies and monthlies, environmental coverage would improve dramatically. In addition, the larger dailies should take their cue from the Oakland *Tribune* and the San Jose *Mercury* by cultivating writers like Fred Garretson and Tom Harris. Otherwise, the Bay Area may be overwhelmed by industrial and governmental inertia.

Case Study: Foreign News (If Anyone Cares)

Now that the world has become a global village—and the moon's surface seems hardly more exotic than a piece of the Mojave desert—it should not be surprising that the American press would devote more space to foreign news. Some students from abroad—who are enrolled in colleges and universities in the United States—still subscribe to their homeland newspapers on the theory that our domestic press has always been too insular to care about the rest of the world. Of course, reading one's homeland newspapers is sensible strategy, whether American newspapers are insular or not. No amount of international news coverage can take the place of a free press and its ability to report and comment on the domestic affairs of its own country. Although foreign students visiting the United States would probably be agreeably surprised by the way the American press now treats foreign news, typical American newspaper coverage is still far from adequate.

Even the most enthusiastic assessment, therefore, does not suggest that foreign news dominates the pages of American newspapers, or even that our press is as internationally minded as those abroad. In one comparison of English and American newspapers (*Journalism Quarterly*, Autumn 1966), Professor Jim Hart of Southern Illinois University found that the slender English papers were more attentive to the world than even the best of the bulky American papers. But the margin was not great.

The proportion of space devoted to foreign news in the American press is no longer scandalously meager. Moreover, leaders like the Los Angeles *Times* and the Washington *Post* are not alone in flavoring their offerings with more foreign news. Professor Hart's study showed that a newspaper on the second level, the Minneapolis *Tribune,* and some that are at least a cut below the *Tribune,* such as the Philadelphia *Inquirer,* gave almost as much of their news space to international affairs as did the *Post.* Thus, it is not uncommon for an average metropolitan daily to carry 300 column inches of foreign news every day.

Bay Area Papers Compared with Others

In proud San Francisco, where cosmopolitanism is supposed to be a way of life and the foreign born are everywhere, one would assume that the major newspapers would devote substantial proportions of

141

DISTRIBUTION OF NEWS, FEATURES AND OPIN|

Newspapers	Local, County, State Politics and Gov't		National Politics and Gov't		International Affairs		Crime, Accidents, Disasters		Ed: Scie F
	Col. In.	%	Col. In.	%	Col. In.	%	Col. In.	%	Co In
Bay Area Papers:									
Oakland *Tribune*	127.5	2.4	115.5	2.1	129.5	2.4	201.0	3.7	432
San Francisco *Chronicle*	123.5	3.1	57.5	1.4	126.5	3.2	335.5	8.4	479
San Francisco *Examiner*	72.5	1.8	151.0	3.7	111.0	2.7	202.0	4.9	319
San Jose *Mercury*	422.0	8.7	147.5	3.0	87.5	1.8	287.0	5.9	527
San Jose *News*	136.5	3.4	160.5	4.0	153.5	3.8	148.0	3.7	273
Comparison Papers:									
Atlanta *Constitution*	252.0	7.9	116.5	3.7	163.5	5.1	72.5	2.3	77
Buffalo *News*	178.5	5.0	182.5	5.1	229.5	6.5	222.5	6.3	274
Los Angeles *Times*	256.5	5.3	230.5	4.7	259.0	5.3	181.0	3.7	263
New York *Times*	474.5	8.1	229.0	3.9	430.5	7.5	102.0	1.7	1831
Toronto *Globe & Mail*	98.5	2.6	158.0	4.1	251.0	6.5	199.5	5.2	127

ᵃ Percentage totals rounded.

their news space to international affairs.[1] But the assumption is not supported by the facts. In preparing the information summarized in Table 9, we first analyzed the contents of single issues of the San Francisco *Chronicle* and *Examiner*, and found surprisingly small percentages of total news space devoted to foreign news. We then examined two other issues of these papers, with similar results.

Next we analyzed the contents of the other three metropolitan dailies published in the Bay Area, first a single issue, then two other issues.[2] The Oakland *Tribune* and the San Jose *Mercury* and *News* were no more sensitive to the need for foreign news than the two San Francisco dailies. We then compared the Bay Area's major dailies with four other dailies published in other parts of the country, and one in Canada. Two of these papers were the New York *Times* and the Los Angeles *Times*. Because it may not seem fair to compare the Bay Area's local papers only with such giants, the other three chosen were less prestigious—less likely to consider themselves newspapers of record—the Atlanta *Constitution*, the Buffalo *News* and the Toronto *Globe and Mail*.

One of our analytical methods gave an advantage to the Bay Area

[1] San Francisco ranks third among major U. S. cities in its percentage of foreign born residents.

[2] All tallies in Table 9 are based on January 9, 1969 editions.

PERS, BY MAJOR SUBJECT AREAS, JANUARY 9, 1969

Inter-alth, ciety	Sports		Amusements		Opinion		Economics, Business, Labor		Miscellaneous		Total Col. Inches	Total %[a]
%	Col. In.	%	Col. In.	%	Col. In.	%	Col. In.	%	Col. In.	%		
27.0	1113.0	20.7	474.0	8.8	342.0	6.4	915.0	17.0	79.5	1.5	5382.0	100
18.0	638.0	16.1	500.5	12.6	413.0	10.4	506.5	12.7	80.5	2.0	3975.0	100
18.0	781.0	19.1	701.0	17.1	318.0	7.8	625.5	15.3	76.0	1.9	4094.0	100
27.0	588.0	12.1	547.5	11.3	166.0	3.4	633.0	13.1	127.5	2.6	4840.0	100
26.1	562.0	13.9	526.0	13.0	326.0	8.1	598.5	14.8	96.0	2.4	4033.0	100
32.0	465.0	14.6	282.5	8.9	291.5	9.1	417.0	13.1	25.0	.08	3180.5	100
26.8	369.0	10.4	387.5	10.9	190.5	5.4	517.5	14.6	48.0	1.4	3552.0	100
23.7	485.0	9.9	714.5	14.6	343.5	7.0	906.5	18.6	82.0	1.7	4878.0	100
19.4	366.0	6.3	162.0	2.8	244.5	4.2	791.0	13.5	87.0	1.5	5855.5	100
16.7	556.0	14.5	185.0	4.8	380.5	9.9	1214.0	31.6	34.0	.09	3844.0	100

dailies, and reduced the foreign news percentages of the New York *Times* and the Los Angeles *Times* considerably (to seven percent and five percent respectively).[3] But the two still remained well above the low levels of the Bay Area papers. No method of juggling and figuring could alter the fact that, either in terms of a percentage of total news space or total column inches, each of the five major Bay Area dailies carried less foreign news than any of the five other papers chosen for comparison. It is not surprising that Bay Area papers carry less foreign news (see International Affairs, Table 9) than the New York *Times* and the Los Angeles *Times*. But less than the Toronto *Globe & Mail*? Less than the Atlanta *Constitution*? Less than the Buffalo *News*?

[3] Instead of placing in the "International Affairs" category the opinion columns that dealt with foreign news and letters-to-the-editor that commented on foreign affairs—the usual practice in such studies—we assigned all opinion columns and letters to the "Opinion" category. This worked to the advantage of the Bay Area's papers, because few of their opinion columns and letters commented on international affairs. Thus exclusion of opinion columns and letters from the "International Affairs" percentages gave the Bay Area papers a better chance of comparing favorably with the New York *Times* and the Los Angeles *Times,* both of which carried many opinion columns and letters on international affairs.

The New York *Times*'s and the Los Angeles *Times*'s percentages in the "National Politics and Government" category were also reduced more than those for the other papers. Both carried many opinion columns and letters on national affairs—considerably more than most other American papers.

What Does the Chronicle Print?

The kind and character of reports that newspapers offer are more important than either the percentages or the column inches devoted to foreign news. With nearly 500,000 subscribers, the *Chronicle* has more than double the circulation of any other Bay Area newspaper. Thus it was appropriate to focus on the quality of foreign coverage provided by the *Chronicle*. We chose the final home edition of January 9, 1969, for the evaluation.[4]

The front page carried stories of a police-student clash at San Francisco State College, a raid on a hippie mansion, and several other eye-catchers. Nearly every story the *Chronicle* featured on page one originated in San Francisco. The exceptions were: one story from Los Angeles, one from Sacramento and a third from Monterey. The front page had no stories that originated outside of California. (One observer pointed out that the *Chronicle*'s policy on departmentalization assigned local news to the early pages and foreign news to later pages.)

Page two, in turn, was almost as parochial as page one. Only a short report, "Winds Kill 2 in Colorado," suggested to readers that there were other climes, other people. Foreign news first appeared on page three—a five-inch report on "Raging Fires in Australia." Another foreign news item turned up on page four, a one-inch story that can be reprinted here in its entirety: "Canadian Prime Minister Pierre Elliot Trudeau missed a session of the Commonwealth Prime Ministers Conference yesterday after coming down with a cold."

Under ordinary circumstances, the record thus far might suggest to anyone who cared about "the world somewhere out there," that he should jettison the *Chronicle* and have a more serious paper delivered—if necessary, flown in daily from the outside. But let us ignore those first four pages, and grant a major premise of *Chronicle* philosophy, i.e., the reader must be given a certain amount of pap so that he will be lured inside to more substantial fare.

There was no foreign news on page five, but on page six the *Chronicle* included a 23-inch story headlined "Witches and Things," about modern witchcraft in Portugal. Above the main head ran a smaller headline: "Lisbon is Talking About."

Such stories represent one of the *Chronicle*'s chief innovations in American journalism. Instead of printing the kind and variety of foreign news that commonly appears in serious newspapers, the editors have instructed their foreign operatives—nearly all of them part-time employees, or "stringers"—to try to determine what people are talking

[4] The record would look somewhat better on a Sunday, when *This World* uses foreign news from some of the wire services.

about over lunch in cities around the world.[5] Judging by the results, these are peculiar lunchtime conversations. For example, the reporters appeared to find that the French never talked about Pompidou, De Gaulle, the Common Market, French glory, or French philosophy; the English never talked about the government's austerity program, the rise of the red-brick universities, taxes or the problem of the pound. In fact, lunchtime conversations over the world seemed startlingly alike. Everyone everywhere was apparently talking only about sex, voodoo, witchcraft, drinking (in India, the City of Trivandrum is talking about "Toddy Tapping"), or some form of eccentric behavior.

Page eight featured another variety of the *Chronicle's* favorite foreign news story, "Trial of Six Opens in Swiss 'Devil Girl' Slaying." It was exactly as long, nine inches, as that day's first conventional foreign item, a page seven story that reported on the plans of Ambassador W. Averell Harriman to leave Paris after months of conducting peace talks.

Other items of foreign news appeared in the January 9 issue, of course, and a few were serious reports. But it is significant that the three longest stories—the only ones running more than 20 inches—reported on witchcraft in Portugal, the fact that 1969 was a lucky year in Japan because it was the "Year of the Cock," and "Bloody Flight from Cuba," a story on the escape from Cuba of 80 rebels, which appeared on page 15. In short, the major foreign news emphasis in the *Chronicle* issue of January 9 was assigned to two items of superstition and one of bloodshed. This was par for a very peculiar course.

The reader should note further the alternative treatments of the Cuba escape story as discussed in the following section of this study. Significantly, the good foreign news story gives a framework for understanding. The mediocre story does not.

The Chronicle and the New York Times News Service

It is not ordinarily considered fair to compare other newspapers with the New York *Times*. The latter does its utmost to provide posterity, as well as current readers, with a full record of each day's events. But there is one justification in comparing the *Chronicle* with the *Times:* the *Chronicle* buys the New York Times News Service, thereby preventing it from being used by any other Bay Area newspaper, except the San Jose *Mercury* and *News*. This means that every day the *Chronicle* receives nearly 30,000 words of the best news, features and opinion

---

[5] Although nearly all of the "Talking About" series are written by *Chronicle* stringers, some are winnowed from news service reports. The item on witchcraft in Portugal was provided by, of all unlikely services, the New York Times News Service. The *Times* did not see fit to publish the story in its own columns.

offerings the *Times* has, most of which the *Times* will publish. The amount of this *Times* material the *Chronicle* uses is determined by the *Chronicle*'s editors.

On January 9, there was some duplication—of a sort—in *Chronicle* and *Times* offerings. For example, the *Chronicle* had the one-paragraph item already mentioned on the Commonwealth Prime Ministers Conference—the one that featured Canadian Prime Minister Trudeau's head cold. The *Times* story on the conference was not about Trudeau's head cold but about one of the most sensitive issues facing the Commonwealth: race relations.

There was not much difference in the length of the *Chronicle* and *Times* stories on the escape from Cuba, but what a difference in substance! Like the *Chronicle* (which used the Los Angeles Times-Washington Post report) the *Times* reported fully on action, shooting and bloodshed. But the last half of the *Times* story placed the bloody event in context. The *Times* reporter offered full details on an airlift that brought Cuban refugees to the United States five times a week as a result of an agreement between the U. S. and Cuba. In operation more than three years, the airlift had already brought in more than 130,000 Cubans. But males between 15 and 26 years, and some technicians and specialists who are older, were not allowed to leave, the *Times* reported. Those who successfully applied for the airlift faced a waiting period of about two years, and could take only a few possessions with them. It was to avoid such restrictions that the fleeing Cubans fought their way to the United States base at Guantanamo. The *Times* story ended with four paragraphs explaining that the U. S. maintains the 45-square-mile base to serve the fleet, and that Castro had spent millions to build a fortified no-man's land on a wide strip of terrain adjoining the base.

The *Chronicle* report was all derring-do. The *Times* story put derring-do in a framework of understanding. The difference called to mind a *Times* editor's explanation of his paper's attitude toward reports of violence: "When other papers cover a murder, it's sensationalism. When we cover a murder, it's sociology." The editor spoke half arrogantly, half in jest, but his statement sketched the *Times*'s policy regarding most news items, and it emphasized a distinct difference between the philosophy of the *Chronicle* and the philosophy of the *Times*.

The dividing line between the *Times*'s coverage of the world and that of all the other Bay Area papers—except the *Chronicle*—is less clear, partly because the other local papers have not adopted the *Chronicle*'s philosophy of titillation as an absolute good. As the table above shows, however, the rest of the Bay Area metropolitan dailies have not extended themselves to expand their readers' knowledge of world events.

Moreover, although they pay lip-service to the ideal of providing background information—i.e., the *Times* story of the fleeing Cubans—as well as action, the background is sparse or nonexistent.

Going through the local papers and matching their foreign news coverage with that of papers which energetically seek to inform their readers about world events is a tedious and depressing exercise. One who undertakes it sees clearly the inadequacy in the performance of most Bay Area newspapers. There must be an explanation that goes beyond merely suggesting that the local editors are either parochial or don't give a damn.

Who Cares to Read Foreign News?

How many readers really care whether newspapers offer a nourishing menu of foreign news? No doubt there are professors of international relations in Bay Area universities who care deeply. It is not much of a leap of the imagination to include other professors and their students, and businessmen and professional men whose work has an international flavor. Add a smattering of Northern Californians who care because of a wide variety of reasons, including some readers who have no more incentive than a laudable curiosity to know how the world is going.

If reader interest is to be a crucial factor, it seems that there are not enough of these persons interested in foreign news to make a decisive difference. We have alluded to the period when the *Chronicle* was trying to become the New York *Times* or *Herald Tribune* of the west. We have mentioned elsewhere the abortive Western Edition of the New York *Times* itself. Both were failures. They failed in part because an insufficient number of readers seemed to care for them.

It is dangerous to attribute these failures solely to their heavy share of foreign news. It is like trying to assign the reason for a failing political campaign—or a successful one—to a single cause. Did Pat Brown fail to be re-elected to the governorship of California because the voters were tired of him? Because he was tired? Did the voters elect Ronald Reagan because he is handsome? Because he has mastered television? Because he is conservative? Because his program appeals to many Californians? Brown was defeated and Reagan was elected, perhaps, for all these reasons—and others.

By the same token, the old, serious *Chronicle* may have failed because it gave so much space to all that dreary foreign news. Today's *Chronicle* may have reached its present level of success because its foreign news is titillating rather than useful. And because its columnists are provocative. And because it is generally entertaining. And . . . on and on.

The fact remains that few Northern Californians seem to clamor for a serious newspaper. This led us to jettison the first title for this chapter: "The Lack of Foreign News in Bay Area Papers, Or Why Northern Californians Don't Know Any Better." A more accurate title might be "The Lack of Foreign News in Bay Area Papers: Who Cares?"

Bruce Brugmann has argued that Bay Area residents have never really had a chance to show whether they would support a quality daily. Neither the old *Chronicle* of the Paul Smith era nor the Western Edition of the New York *Times* was given sufficient resources to succeed, he maintains. His position is debatable, at least, but we do not propose to contest it further here. Let Brugmann's argument comfort those San Franciscans who are too proud of their city ever to believe that it refuses to embrace quality.

Conclusion

The great question that remains is why the many capable journalists we have cannot lift Bay Area journalism above mediocrity. If we ever had doubts that local journalism *is* mediocre, they were dispelled during our interviews with reporters and editors. One was quite proud of his paper, a few were complacent, but the great majority were dissatisfied with—and often even contemptuous of—significant aspects of their own papers. As for the many readers with whom we discussed local journalism, nearly all were overwhelmingly negative about the papers they read. When one of the authors began to mention to a World Affairs Council audience that a critique of the Bay Area press would soon be published, he was interrupted by a burst of applause that was surprising in its intensity.

The answer to the question of why the Bay Area does not have a great daily newspaper, or even one of undisputed high quality, begins quite simply but becomes exceedingly complicated. The first necessity is an owner who is determined to produce a great paper and knows how to go about it. This is the most important factor, but there are others. The market for the paper must be large enough to provide revenues enabling the owner to pay for a quality product. The community served by the paper must be large. The intellectual level must be such that the readers will feel rewarded by an informative paper, rather than repelled by it. The effort to set the paper on the path toward greatness must be properly timed. For example, the current period of recession or near-recession coupled with inflation (1969–1970) might be a ruinous time to attempt to convert a mediocre paper into a great one.

All these factors are so difficult to mesh in one locale at one time that the creation of a great newspaper might be deemed an accident rather than a considered policy. And, indeed, considering how few of the 1,764 daily newspapers in the United States are of high quality, that may be a reasonable conclusion. Nevertheless, publication in New York, Washington or Chicago is not a prerequisite for obtaining the income necessary to accomplish the task. In the 10 years that he has been publisher of the Los Angeles *Times,* Otis Chandler has transformed it from a family trumpet to one of the four or five best newspapers in the United States. In relatively small St. Petersburg, Florida, Nelson Poynter has been so serious and intelligent about informing his audience that his St. Petersburg *Times* must be ranked with fine newspapers published in much larger cities. The Louisville *Courier-Journal,* which is also published in a relatively small city and in a poor state, is deservedly ranked on nearly every list of great newspapers.

We cannot know whether all the factors listed above will ever be combined so that the Bay Area can produce a great paper. Certainly, we must await the coming of a publisher whose first purpose is quality, whose vision is sharp enough to recognize it, and who works for high profits only because they enable him to provide a more significant public service. (The hard-headed publishers who treat newspapers like any other business have a right to snort derisively at such a prescription. They also have the unquestioned right to milk their newspaper businesses of profits, leaving nothing to improve the product. They are wrong only because they seem to think we should respect them for such performances.)

Even in the absence of an ideal publisher, Bay Area newspapers can be improved markedly. Let us suggest two steps.

First, pay scales for reporters and editors should be raised dramatically to attract and retain first-rate talent. The experience of the Los Angeles *Times,* which lured fine journalists from high-paying magazines by paying them better, suggests what a strong salary scale can accomplish. The list in Appendix II of guild scale minimums (and we are aware that some journalists are paid above minimum scale) indicates that reporters on Bay Area metropolitan papers are being paid comfortably but not professionally. This is a period when top reporters on great papers may earn $25,000 to $35,000, with bureau chiefs earning more. Too many Bay Area editors do not recruit actively. They sit back and riffle through a stack of letters from people who want to come to California, selecting one who looks promising—and who doesn't expect much money.

A former editor said that he was

constantly flooded with job applications from those who want to come to California at almost any pay scale. This helps to keep pay scales down, despite the upward influence of the guild on all Bay Area newspaper salaries. But you would still find, I would guess, that some of the non-guild papers still pay atrociously, a condition that has always influenced the quality of newspapering in the Bay Area.

Most Bay Area newspapers must take the second step of disentangling themselves from local Establishments. One knowledgeable local critic chided us for worrying unduly about the penchant of publishers for making money, and asserted that we should pay attention to the "publishers' real concerns—running their communities."

That brings us to an important consideration: the stance of Bay Area newspapers. The press is the only business institution specifically mentioned in the Bill of Rights, and thereby given a degree of protection from government regulation. This means, of course, that the founding fathers envisioned the press as a check upon government. For this function to be performed effectively, the modern political reporter must do much more than question officials in an abrasive manner, or rub two politicians together to produce newsworthy sparks. The reporter must recognize that we live in the age, not of just a military-industrial complex, but of a government-industrial-labor-education complex. He must be alert to the powerful inducements often employed to lure the communications industries into equal and tranquil partnership with the complexes.

The Skeptical Adversary

Because government seldom constructs its own offices, builds roads, develops parks, writes textbooks, or directly carries on the myriad other activities of modern governance, government has a multitude of inextricable links to business and to all the other pivotal institutions of society that do perform these tasks for government. Professional journalists must serve as adversaries to this system—not belligerently, but questioningly and skeptically.

How well does Bay Area journalism perform this task? To answer the question, one need only look at the destruction of the local environment, the pollution of everything from air to human relationships and at the timidity of the press in failing to expose the contaminators.

At the risk of oversimplification, this comment by Arnold Elkind, chairman of the National Commission on Product Safety, can stand for a whole catalogue of inadequate reporting:

> The news media to whom our records and hearings are available have generally not availed themselves of the opportunity to alert the public to product hazards. With few exceptions, they have deleted brand names and identifying information from reports about product hazards.

This reportorial failure is of crucial importance. Not only is the press the sole knowledgeable adversary to government, but also it is the primary source of the contemporary information with which we organize our lives. We can know very little: there is not much that the citizen can be sure of through direct experience and observation. The world is too big and complex, and our daily paths in it are too narrow and limited—from home to office or classroom, to a store, to club or restaurant or theater, then back home again—for us ever to see and experience more than a tiny sample of the world. We depend upon the press—and radio and television, of course—to provide us with the vast majority of what we understand about contemporary affairs. The information they give us is synthetic—we do not know it at first-hand—but we depend upon it. We have no other choice.

Another problem is the fragmenting of traditional newspaper reporting, which, as one reader said,

> contributes directly and continuously to the inability of newspapers to confront the problems of our times and communities until they are so clear that University students force us to confront them.

In a country like the United States it is especially necessary for the press to recognize its own importance. As James Madison said,

> Knowledge will forever govern ignorance, and a people who mean to be their own governors must arm themselves with the power knowledge gives. Popular government without popular information or the means of acquiring it is but a prologue to a farce, or a tragedy, or perhaps both.

It is especially important that the Bay Area press recognize its responsibility. It is essential that Bay Area editors and publishers commit themselves, not only to slashing at those few politicians who arouse their anger, but also to a role of *speaking truth to power*. If significant power resides in the Pacific Gas and Electric Co., or Pacific Telephone and Telegraph, or Stanford University, or the University of California —and surely it does—the only honest and valuable journalism must confront these power centers with the same stance that is struck before political and governmental power.

Further, in addition to practicing confrontation, the papers need to develop depth and breadth of view both in judgment and in performance.

Shortcomings and Future Directions

In this book we have attempted to point out some of the strengths and shortcomings of Bay Area newspapers. Publishers in the nine-county area have to grapple with every important print media problem and development in the country today. The directions taken by Bay Area newspapers in the next few years should be accurate indicators of what we can expect from newspapers throughout the United States.

Suburban papers will decide whether it is more profitable to concentrate on local news—as is the case in Berkeley and some of the smaller communities in Contra Costa County—or to provide a complete news package, in competition with the metropolitan dailies—as is now the case in San Mateo, Richmond and Vallejo. What will be the role of the underground press, of the semiunderground weeklies and monthlies such as *Freedom News* and the *Bay Guardian?* Answers to these questions will also probably emerge in the next few years.

We have tried to show both the good and bad aspects of joint operating agreements; the successes and failures of the suburban dailies; the solid contributions and questionable extremism of the weeklies and undergrounds. We have commended some papers and criticized others. Our overriding impression of the whole of the Bay Area press can be expressed simply:

We are in a period of revolution. If most of the journalists in the Bay Area, and especially the proprietors of Bay Area papers, think that their present performance is sufficient unto the needs of the hour, then they do not know what time it is.

APPENDICES

APPENDIX I

Bay Area Newspapers:
A. Dailies
(in decreasing order of circulation)

Source: *Editor and Publisher International Yearbook 1969*

Legend: m = morning
  e = evening
  S = Sunday

Name of Newspaper	County of Publication	Circulation	Publisher
San Francisco *Chronicle* (mS)	San Francisco	480,233	Charles de Young Thieriot
Oakland *Tribune* (eS)	Alameda	225,038	William F. Knowland
San Francisco *Examiner* (eS)	San Francisco	208,023	Charles L. Gould
San Jose *Mercury* (mS)	Santa Clara	126,382	B. H. Ridder
San Jose *News* (eS)	Santa Clara	75,531	B. H. Ridder
Santa Rosa *Press-Democrat* (eS)	Sonoma	45,504	Mrs. E. L. Finley
San Mateo *Times* (e)	San Mateo	45,394	J. Hart Clinton
Palo Alto *Times* (e)	Santa Clara	44,520	Charles T. Tyler
San Rafael *Independent-Journal* (e)	Marin	43,649	Wishard A. Brown
Richmond *Independent* (e)	Contra Costa	36,170	Warren Brown, Jr.
Hayward *Review* (eS)	Alameda	35,510	Floyd L. Sparks
Vallejo (morning) *Times-Herald* (mS)	Solano	29,219	Luther E. Gibson
Contra Costa *Times and Green Sheet* (eS)	Contra Costa	23,001	Dean S. Lesher
Redwood City *Tribune* (e)	San Mateo	21,923	Frank J. O'Neill
Napa *Register* (e)	Napa	16,992	J. V. Brenner
Berkeley *Gazette* (m)	Alameda	14,448	Warren Brown, Jr.
Fremont *News-Register* (m)	Alameda	9,618	Abraham Kofman
Concord *Daily Transcript* (e)	Contra Costa	9,355	Dean S. Lesher
Fairfield-Suisun *Daily Republic* (eS)	Solano	9,282	Don R. Hancock
San Leandro *Morning News* (m)	Alameda	9,205	Abraham Kofman
Alameda *Times-Star* (m)	Alameda	8,897	Abraham Kofman
Antioch *Ledger* (e)	Contra Costa	8,737	Dean S. Lesher
Livermore *Herald and News* (m)	Alameda	7,896	Floyd L. Sparks
Fremont *Argus* (m)	Alameda	7,262	Floyd L. Sparks
Petaluma *Argus-Courier* (e)	Sonoma	6,942	Phil Swift
Pittsburg *Post-Dispatch* (e)	Contra Costa	6,705	Mrs. T. R. Bishop
Martinez *Morning News-Gazette* (m)	Contra Costa	3,200	Luther E. Gibson
Gilroy *Evening Dispatch* (e)	Santa Clara	3,166	George R. Kane

Bay Area Newspapers:
B. Weeklies, Bi-Weeklies, Monthlies
(alphabetically by counties)

Source: *Editor and Publisher International Yearbook 1969* and local inquiries. To obtain circulation figures on all weeklies, bi-weeklies and monthlies would have been beyond the scope of this project, and was not attempted. The *Yearbook* noted above is a useful source of information for those newspapers included in its listings.

Name of Newspaper	County of Publication	Day of Issue	Publisher
Albany *Times*	Alameda	Wed.	Ila Mae Wilson
Berkeley *Barb*	Alameda	Thurs.	Max Scheer
Berkeley *Tribe*	Alameda	Thurs.	Red Mountain Tribe, Inc.
Black Panther	Alameda	Sat.	Black Panthers
California Voice (Oakland)	Alameda	Fri.	E. A. Daly
Castro Valley *Reporter*	Alameda	Thurs.	Floyd L. Sparks
Freedom News	Alameda	monthly	Elizabeth Segal
Jornal Portugues	Alameda	Thurs.	Alberto S. Lemos
Montclarion	Alameda	Wed.	Fredric Graeser
Neighborhood Journal	Alameda	Wed.	Peter Victor
Oakland *Observer*	Alameda	Sat.	Marion G. Tibbits
Piedmonter	Alameda	Wed.	E. Clayton Snyder
Pleasanton *Times*	Alameda	Wed.	John B. Edwards
The Post (Berkeley)	Alameda	Thurs.	Thomas L. Berkley
San Lorenzo *Sun-Journal*	Alameda	Thurs.	Floyd L. Sparks
Union City *Leader*	Alameda	Thurs.	Richard L. Folger
Voz de Portugal (Hayward)	Alameda	1st, 14th, 21st of the month	Gilberto L. Aguiar
Brentwood *News*	Contra Costa	Thurs.	William H. Brewer
Concord *Journal*	Contra Costa	Thurs.	L. E. Stoddard
Contra Costa *News Register* (Walnut Creek)	Contra Costa	Tues. & Fri.	Ruth E. Davidson
Crockett *American*	Contra Costa	Thurs.	Andrew M. Peters
Diablo Valley *News*	Contra Costa	Thurs.	E. C. & R. V. Frates, Dr. C. J. Smith
El Cerrito *Journal*	Contra Costa	Wed.	Frank J. Maloney
El Sobrante *Herald Bee Press*	Contra Costa	Thurs.	I. Eddie Galli
Lafayette *Sun*	Contra Costa	Fri.	Dean S. Lesher
Orinda *Sun*	Contra Costa	Fri.	Dean S. Lesher
Pinole-Hercules *News*	Contra Costa	Thurs.	Andrew M. Peters
Pleasant Hill *Post*	Contra Costa	Thurs.	L. E. Stoddard
Pleasant Hill *Sun*	Contra Costa	Fri.	Dean S. Lesher

158

Name of Newspaper	County of Publication	Day of Issue	Publisher
San Pablo *News*	Contra Costa	Wed.	Frank J. Maloney
Tri-City News (Rodeo)	Contra Costa	Fri.	Andrew M. Peters
Valley Pioneer (Danville)	Contra Costa	Wed.	R. Semmes Gordon
Walnut Creek *Sun*	Contra Costa	Fri.	Dean S. Lesher
Walnut Kernal	Contra Costa	Thurs.	L. E. Stoddard
Corte Madera-Larkspur *Courier*	Marin	Wed.	John Luc
Corte Madera *Times-Herald Tribune*	Marin	Wed.	Frank Marchi
Ebb Tide (Tiburon)	Marin	Wed.	John Luc
Fairfax-San Anselmo *Reporter-Sun*	Marin	Wed.	Peter Edwards
Larkspur-Corte Madera *Times-Herald-Tribune*	Marin	Wed.	Frank Marchi
Mill Valley *News-Herald-Tribune*	Marin	Wed.	Frank Marchi
Mill Valley *Record*	Marin	Wed.	Edward M. Mills & Katharine S. Mills
Novato *Advance*	Marin	Wed.	George A. Barnwell
Pacific Sun (San Rafael)	Marin	Thurs.	Stephen McNamara
Point Reyes *Light*	Marin	Thurs.	Don De Wolf
Ross Valley *Times-Herald-Tribune*	Marin	Wed.	Frank Marchi
San Rafael *Herald-Tribune*	Marin	Wed.	Wayne Swift
Sausalito *News-Herald-Tribune*	Marin	Wed.	Harry Johnson
Terra Linda *News*	Marin	Wed.	Eric C. Colby
Tiburon *Pelican-Herald-Tribune*	Marin	Wed	Frank Marchi
St. Helena *Star*	Napa	Thurs.	Starr Baldwin
The Weekly Calistogan	Napa	Thurs.	Ted J. Libby
Yountsville *Weekly News*	Napa	Thurs.	John A. Nemes
Bien	San Francisco	Thurs.	Barbara R. Stribolt
Chinese Pacific Weekly	San Francisco	Thurs.	Gilbert Woo
Dock of the Bay (incorporated the *Peninsula Observer*)	San Francisco	Sat.	Bay Area Media Network
Good Times	San Francisco	Wed.	Waller Press
Jewish Community Bulletin	San Francisco	Fri.	Eugene J. Block
Monitor	San Francisco	Thurs.	Roman Catholic Archbishop of S.F.
The Movement	San Francisco	monthly	The Movement
Northern California Industrial and Business News	San Francisco	alternate Mon.	
Richmond *Banner*	San Francisco	Fri.	Frances C. Trimble
Rolling Stone	San Francisco	bi-weekly	Straight Arrow Pub.
San Francisco *Bay Guardian*	San Francisco	monthly	Bruce Brugmann

Name of Newspaper	County of Publication	Day of Issue	Publisher
San Francisco *Progress*	San Francisco	Wed. & Sat.	Henry J. Budde
Sun Reporter	San Francisco	Thurs.	Carlton B. Goodlett, M.D.
Swiss Journal	San Francisco	Wed.	Mario Muschi
Vestkusten	San Francisco	Thurs.	Karin W. Person
Belmont *Courier-Bulletin*	San Mateo	Wed.	L. K. Rhodes
Brisbane *Bee-Democrat*	San Mateo	Thurs.	Logan Franklin
Burlingame *Advance-Star*	San Mateo	Wed. & Sat.	Edwin W. Rice
Coastside Chronicle (Pacifica)	San Mateo	Wed.	Alton I. Cloud
Foster City *Progress*	San Mateo	Wed.	R. M. Buren
Half Moon Bay *Review*	San Mateo	Thurs.	Edward M. Bauer, Jr.
Menlo-Atherton *Recorder*	San Mateo	Wed.	Richard Nowels
Millbrae *Sun and Leader*	San Mateo	Wed.	Anne Loftus
North County Post	San Mateo	Wed.	J. Hart Clinton
Pacifica *Tribune*	San Mateo	Wed.	William A. Drake & Margaret B. Drake
The Record and Westlake Times (Daly City)	San Mateo	Wed. & Fri.	Logan Franklin
San Bruno *Herald and Recorder-Progress*	San Mateo	Wed. & Thurs.	Alton I. Cloud
San Carlos *Enquirer*	San Mateo	Wed.	A. H. Dorinson
San Mateo County *Union Gazette*	San Mateo	Mon.	A. J. Remmenga, Gen. Ma:
San Mateo *Post*	San Mateo	Wed.	J. Hart Clinton
South San Francisco *Enterprise-Journal*	San Mateo	Wed. & Fri.	Logan Franklin
Almaden-Cambrian *Sun Guide*	Santa Clara	Wed.	Morton I. Levine
Cambrian Weekly News (San Jose)	Santa Clara	Wed.	Wilton von Gease
Campbell *Press*	Santa Clara	Wed.	George Vierhus
Cupertino *Courier*	Santa Clara	Wed.	David MacKenzie & William J. Norton
East San Jose *Sun*	Santa Clara	Wed.	Morton I. Levine
Los Gatos *Times-Observer*	Santa Clara	Tues., Thurs.	George R. Kane
Milpitas *Post*	Santa Clara	Wed.	Morton I. Levine
Morgan Hill *Times* and San Martin *News*	Santa Clara	Thurs.	Ralph W. Slauter
North San Jose *Sun*	Santa Clara	Wed.	Morton I. Levine
San Jose *Sun*	Santa Clara	Wed.	Morton I. Levine
South San Jose *Sun-Graphic*	Santa Clara	Wed.	Morton I. Levine
Sunnyvale *Scribe*	Santa Clara	Thurs.	David MacKenzie & William J. Norton
Town Crier (Los Altos)	Santa Clara	Wed.	David MacKenzie & William J. Norton

ıme of ewspaper	County of Publication	Day of Issue	Publisher
illow Glen Sun-Times (San Jose)	Santa Clara	Wed.	Morton I. Levine
nicia Herald	Solano	Thurs.	Thomas M. Banks
he Benician	Solano	Thurs.	H. D. Frane
xon Tribune	Solano	Thurs.	Frederic N. Dunnicliff
ver News-Herald & Isleton Journal	Solano	Wed.	Esther T. Pierce
caville Reporter	Solano	Mon. & Thurs.	John Rico
overdale Reveille	Sonoma	Thurs.	Jerome J. Tupy & Terrance L. Thompson
eyserville Press	Sonoma	Thurs.	Jerome J. Tupy & Terrance L. Thompson
ealdsburg Tribune, Enterprise & Scimitar	Sonoma	Thurs.	Dean Dunnicliff
ews-Herald (Santa Rosa)	Sonoma	Wed.	George R. Chase
noma County Herald-Recorder	Sonoma	Mon., Wed., Fri.	Dale Sipe
noma Index-Tribune	Sonoma	Thurs.	Robert M. Lynch
imes (Sebastopol)	Sonoma	Thurs.	Ernest V. Joiner
he World (Cotati)	Sonoma	Wed.	Kvan, Inc.
he World (Rohnert Park)	Sonoma	Wed.	Kvan, Inc.

APPENDIX II

Top Minimum Weekly Salaries for Reporters and Photographers in Selected Newspapers:

American Newspaper Guild Contracts as of August 1, 1970
(Figures supplied by the American Newspaper Guild)

Name of Newspaper	Minimum	After
Washington *Post*	$263.25	5 yrs
Washington *News*	260.00	5 yrs
NY *Times*	ª255.25	2 yrs
Washington *Star*	249.50	4 yrs
Chicago *Sun-Times & News* (2)	246.92	5 yrs
NY *News*	ᵇ242.30	6 yrs
ᵈOakland *Tribune*	240.75	6 yrs
Sacramento *Bee*	240.75	6 yrs
ᵈSan Francisco *Chronicle & Examiner* (2)	240.75	6 yrs
St. Louis *Post-Dispatch*	240.00	5 yrs
NY *Post*	ᶜ239.20	4 yrs
ᵈSan Jose *Mercury & News* (2)	233.59	6 yrs
Stockton *Record*	233.00	6 yrs
Sacramento *Union*	230.83	6 yrs
ᵈRichmond (Cal.) *Independent*	230.00	6 yrs
ᵈSanta Rosa *Press-Democrat*	230.00	6 yrs
ᵈVallejo *Times-Herald*	230.00	6 yrs
St. Louis *Globe-Democrat*	229.00	5 yrs
ᵈSan Mateo *Times*	226.16	6 yrs
Cleveland *Plain Dealer*	225.00	4 yrs
Detroit *Free Press*	222.35	4 yrs
Pittsburgh *Post-Gazette*	220.00	4 yrs
Baltimore *Sun & Evening Sun* (2)	220.00	5 yrs
Toledo *Blade & Times* (2)	219.50	4 yrs
East St. Louis: *Metro E. Journal*	217.60	5 yrs
Seattle *Post-Intelligencer*	215.00	5 yrs
Seattle *Times*	215.00	5 yrs
Gary *Post-Tribune*	213.35	5 yrs
Long Beach *Independent & Press-Telegram* (2)	208.80	5 yrs
San Diego *Union & Tribune* (3)	205.75	6 yrs
NY: Long Island *Press*	200.00	3 yrs
Vancouver *Sun & Province* (2)	193.63	5 yrs
Bakersfield *Californian*	192.50	5 yrs
Toronto *Globe & Mail*	192.00	5 yrs
Chattanooga *Times*	186.00	5 yrs
Fall River *Herald-News*	180.00	4 yrs
San Pedro *News-Pilot*	176.80	5 yrs
Los Angeles *Herald-Examiner*	174.80	5 yrs

162

Name of Newspaper	Minimum	After
San Antonio *Light*	170.01	5 yrs
Sioux City *Journal*	162.75	4 yrs
Terre Haute *Tribune & Star* (2)	156.50	5 yrs
Alexandria *Gazette*	135.00	6 yrs
Lowell *Sun*	134.00	5 yrs

a Includes $5.25 cost-of-living increase.
b Includes $5.00 cost-of-living increase.
c Includes $4.90 cost-of-living increase.
d Bay Area newspapers.

Note: A contract signed in San Francisco in November 1970, like a number of others signed recently, requires that after five or six years of experience, reporters and photographers will be paid more than $300 a week, or about $16,000 a year. In the near future, additional new contracts will increase the minimums paid by other publishers in large metropolitan areas. It is assumed, however, that the long-term salary relationships shown above will not be changed appreciably.

Comparative Treatment of Six National News Items
February 17–March 4, 1969

Newspaper and story	Total column inches	No. of days on first four pages	No. of days out of 14 story run	% of headlines "biased"[a]
VIETNAM				
New York *Times*	916	9	14	.10
Oakland *Tribune* . . .	570	14	14	.45
San Francisco *Examiner* .	439	11	14	.39
San Jose *Mercury*	402	11	14	.41
San Francisco *Chronicle* .	388	5	14	.36
Berkeley *Gazette*	194	10	12	.47
Vallejo *Times-Herald* . .	171	7	10	.33
MID-EAST CRISIS				
New York *Times*	815	13	14	.09
Oakland *Tribune*	337	9	14	.11
San Francisco *Chronicle* .	322	6	13	.20
San Francisco *Examiner* .	296	7	14	.30
San Jose *Mercury*	296	4	13	.25
Berkeley *Gazette*	145	9	11	.30
Vallego *Times-Herald* . .	73	5	6	.00
CONGRESS				
New York *Times*	775	10	14	.04
San Francisco *Examiner* .	338	9	11	.36
Oakland *Tribune*	246	9	12	.30
San Francisco *Chronicle* .	222	5	14	.27
Berkeley *Gazette*	177	6	7	.17
San Jose *Mercury*	139	2	12	.38
Vallejo *Times-Herald* . .	103	1	9	.27
THE PRESIDENT				
New York *Times*	1600	11	14	.04
San Francisco *Examiner* .	776	13	14	.35
Oakland *Tribune* . . .	671	13	14	.29
San Jose *Mercury*	589	7	14	.17
San Francisco *Chronicle* .	538	8	14	.36
Vallejo *Times-Herald* . .	255	7	10	.00
Berkeley *Gazette*	159	5	8	.40

Newspaper and story	Total column inches	No. of days on first four pages	No. of days out of 14 story run	% of headlines "biased"[a]
COLD WAR				
New York *Times*	832	12	14	.08
San Francisco *Chronicle* . .	332	6	13	.35
San Jose *Mercury*	291	8	14	.42
Oakland *Tribune*	273	11	13	.40
San Francisco *Examiner* .	216	10	13	.20
Berkeley *Gazette*	147	7	11	.25
Vallejo *Times-Herald* . .	99	2	6	.28
PRESIDIO MUTINY[b]				
San Francisco *Chronicle* .	246	4	10	.15
San Francisco *Examiner* .	229	0	10	.36
San Jose *Mercury* . . .	80	1	7	.14
Oakland *Tribune*	68	0	6	.28
Vallejo *Times-Herald* . .	57	0	6	.00
Berkeley *Gazette*	28	1	3	.00

[a] In our working definition, a biased headline is one that contains a value-laden word for which an equivalent and less value-laden word could have been substituted. For example in headlining a murder story, "slaughter" is more value-laden than "kill."

[b] Data for the New York *Times* are not included, because the *Times* ran nothing on the mutiny during the 14-day period of analysis.

APPENDIX IV

Newspaper Source Materials Used in the Study

A. MAJOR TOPICS EXAMINED AND WHY THEY WERE CHOSEN FOR QUALITATIVE ANALYSIS

Topic or Category	Notes on Bases for Selection
Goals and Performance	These qualitative topics revealed basic information concerning every paper under study, and helped us formulate an overview of each one. Time periods covered were related to the development of major stories.
Sunday Papers	The personality of a Sunday paper may be quite different from that of the daily. Further, Sunday reading offers the rare opportunity for some busy people to follow news developments and to reflect on what they read.
Weeklies	Because every sizeable community has one, the weekly has an important role to play in community awareness and local politics. Some of the best journalism in the Bay Area is found in weeklies.
Monthlies	The world of underground journalism is largely that of monthlies. Since the Bay Area is in the forefront of the underground movement, we thought it appropriate to take at least a brief look at selected monthlies.
Opinion Columns	An editor's choice of syndicated material provides a useful clue in evaluating the quality of the editorial page. The nature of the home-grown columns can also indicate a newspaper's involvement with the community and the editor's own philosophy of newspapering.
Student Unrest	This was chosen for study because it comprises one of the most important local stories that all of the papers in the sample could be expected to cover on their own, apart from the wire services.
Regional Organization and the Environmental Crisis	This topic was particularly appropriate for a regionwide study of newspaper performance. In addition, the environmental story was unusually significant because the Bay conservation commission was strengthened and made permanent in 1969. Local newspapers could be expected to have their own staff members covering the story.

166

Topic or Category	*Notes on Bases for Selection*
Foreign News	This material is usually the most neglected part of a newspaper's coverage. Moreover, the topic permits comparisons with newspapers outside the Bay Area, an examination that cannot be performed with local news. Finally, it seemed likely that important differences on this score might be found among the five major Bay Area papers.
	For the group of comparison papers, the New York *Times* and the Los Angeles *Times* were chosen as embodying accepted standards of quality; the other three were selected because they serve central cities that are roughly the same size as the larger Bay Area cities, because they are usually *not* listed among the "great" papers in the United States (as the New York *Times* and the Los Angeles *Times* usually are), and because they are based in metropolitan areas.
	No particular significance is attached to the date of January 9, 1969. Comparable editions of all papers under scrutiny were available for that date.

B. SUMMARY OF TOPICS, NEWSPAPERS AND DATES
IN THE QUALITATIVE DISCUSSION

Topic	*Newspaper*	*Dates*
Goals and Performance	Sample includes: San Francisco *Chronicle* San Francisco *Examiner* Oakland *Tribune* San Jose *Mercury* and *News* San Mateo *Times* Berkeley *Gazette* Vallejo *Times-Herald* Palo Alto *Times* Santa Rosa *Press-Democrat*	Period between December 23, 1968 and March 4, 1969

Sunday Papers	All those in the 9-county area:
	Sunday San Francisco
	  Examiner and Chronicle
	Sunday San Jose *Mercury-
	  News*
	Sunday Oakland *Tribune*
	Sunday Santa Rosa *Press-
	  Democrat*
	Sunday Vallejo *Times-
	  Herald*
	Sunday Hayward *Review*
		Period between
		December 23, 1968
		and March 4, 1969

Weeklies	Nominated from among 96 weeklies in the Bay Area	Period between December 23, 1968 and March 4, 1969
Monthlies	Nominated as among the best: *Bay Guardian* *Plain Rapper* *Freedom News*	Period between December 23, 1968 and March 4, 1969
Opinion Columns (editorial page and the page opposite)	Same sample as for "Goals and Performance" study: San Francisco *Chronicle* San Francisco *Examiner* Oakland *Tribune* San Jose *Mercury* and *News* San Mateo *Times* Berkeley *Gazette* Vallejo *Times-Herald* Palo Alto *Times* Santa Rosa *Press-Democrat*	Period between December 23, 1968 and March 4, 1969

Topic	Newspaper	Dates
Student Unrest	Same sample as for "Goals and Performance" study, used for nonquantitative analysis	Eighteen weeks in period during December 1968 through April 1969
Regional Organization and the Environmental Crisis	Same sample as for "Goals and Performance" study, used for nonquantitative analysis	Period between December 23, 1968 and March 4, 1969
Foreign News	San Francisco *Chronicle* San Francisco *Examiner* Oakland *Tribune* San Jose *Mercury* and *News* New York *Times* Los Angeles *Times* Atlanta *Constitution* Buffalo *News* Toronto *Globe & Mail*	January 9, 1969

C. SOME QUANTITATIVE ANALYSES

Topics for Tables	*Notes on Bases for Selection*
News Judgment, Front-Page Stories: Table 1	Variations in the news judgment of editors, as seen in the contents of their papers' front pages, demonstrate how the reader's perception of the world can be affected. We paired two sets of newspapers (the *Mercury* and the *Chronicle*; the *Tribune* and the *Examiner*), for three dates chosen at random, to see whether distinctive differences in content would show up. They did.
Cranston-Rafferty Race: Table 2	The *Tribune*'s treatment of this story was used to illustrate the way political philosophy can affect coverage in terms of column inches.
Student Unrest, the Vietnam War and the Pueblo Investigation: Tables 3, 4 and 5	These three topics were all issues of major importance during the observation period of February 17 through March 4, 1969. The treatment of a local, a national and an international issue during this period thus made meaningful column inch comparisons possible. To simplify quantitative comparisons during the two-week sample period, six Bay Area papers (instead of the 10 used in the Major Topics examination in section A) were followed for the local student unrest story. To these six, the New York *Times* was added for comparison in the Pueblo and Vietnam stories.
Campus Problems and the U. C. Regents' Meeting: Table 6	January 18, 1969, the day after the Regents' meeting, presented an opportunity for observing the way in which Bay Area papers covered a substantive event closely related to the student unrest story. It was also a Saturday, when the Santa Rosa *Press-Democrat* does not publish an edition. Thus, the overall comparisons include nine instead of 10 Bay Area papers.
Treatment of Santa Barbara Oil Leak and Sirhan Trial: Tables 7 and 8	The same six local papers and the New York *Times* were compared during the two-week period for quantitative treatment to discern news judgments concerning a story of statewide ecological importance and one of national political importance.

Topics for Tables	Notes on Bases for Selection
Distribution of News, Features and Opinion: Table 9	This tally was, of course, closely linked with the examination of foreign news described in section A. The 10 additional categories shown in Table 9 permitted substantial comparisons between the performance of the five major Bay Area papers and the five out-of-state papers.
Treatment of Six National News Items: Appendix III	The tally expanded on the Vietnam war treatment noted above. The same newspapers were examined on the same dates, with the addition of two topics of international importance: the Mid-East crisis and the cold war, and three of national importance: the President, the Congress and the Presidio mutiny story.

D. SUMMARY OF TOPICS, NEWSPAPERS AND DATES IN THE QUANTITATIVE STUDY

Topic	Newspaper	Dates
Column Inches on Cranston-Rafferty Race	Oakland *Tribune*	October 1968
Column Inches on Student Unrest	Berkeley *Gazette* San Francisco *Chronicle* Oakland *Tribune* San Francisco *Examiner* San Jose *Mercury* Vallejo *Times-Herald*	February 17– March 4, 1969
Column Inches on Vietnam War	New York *Times* Oakland *Tribune* San Francisco *Examiner* San Jose *Mercury* San Francisco *Chronicle* Berkeley *Gazette* Vallejo *Times-Herald*	February 17– March 4, 1969
Column Inches on Pueblo Investigation	New York *Times* San Jose *Mercury* Vallejo *Times-Herald* San Francisco *Examiner* Oakland *Tribune* San Francisco *Chronicle* Berkeley *Gazette*	February 17– March 4, 1969

Topic	Newspaper	Dates
Column Inches on Campus Problems and the U. C. Regents' Meeting	San Francisco *Chronicle* San Jose *News* San Francisco *Examiner* Oakland *Tribune* Berkeley *Gazette* Vallejo *Times-Herald* San Jose *Mercury* San Mateo *Times* Palo Alto *Times*	January 18, 1969
Treatment of Oil Leak	San Francisco *Chronicle* San Jose *Mercury* New York *Times* Vallejo *Times-Herald* Oakland *Tribune* San Francisco *Examiner* Berkeley *Gazette*	February 17– March 4, 1969
Treatment of Sirhan Trial	New York *Times* San Jose *Mercury* San Francisco *Chronicle* Vallejo *Times-Herald* Oakland *Tribune* San Francisco *Examiner* Berkeley *Gazette*	March 4, 1969 February 17–
Distribution of News, Features and Opinion	Atlanta *Constitution* Buffalo *News* Los Angeles *Times* New York *Times* Oakland *Tribune* San Francisco *Chronicle* San Francisco *Examiner* San Jose *Mercury* San Jose *News* Toronto *Globe & Mail*	January 9, 1969
Treatment of Six National News Items	New York *Times*[a] Oakland *Tribune* San Francisco *Examiner* San Jose *Mercury* San Francisco *Chronicle* Berkeley *Gazette* Vallejo *Times-Herald*	February 17– March 4, 1969

[a] Included in all tallies except that for the Presidio mutiny, because the *Times* did not use that story during the period studied.

3*m*-2,'71 (P1022)